NAVAJO
AND HOPI
WEAVING
TECHNIQUES

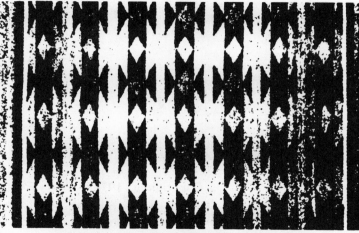

NAVAJO AND HOPI WEAVING TECHNIQUES

Mary Pendleton

Studio Vista

Studio Vista
Cassell and Collier Macmillan Publishers Limited
35 Red Lion Square, London WC1R 4SG

ISBN 0 289 70558 4

First published in Great Britain in 1974

Printed in the United States of America

In memory of my mother, Marie Reddick, who was always so proud of her children's accomplishments.

In memory of my sister, Avis Murphy, whose love of music and abilities at the keyboard gave pleasure to so many.

Preface

I have been a weaver for over twenty-five years. My first weaving years were spent in Ohio, and it was not until I came west, about 1953, that I really got interested in the Indian weaving techniques. Since moving to Sedona, Arizona, in 1958 I have been involved with the Indian craftsmen.

Because of the tremendous interest in Navajo weaving and the lack of information regarding it, I began my first writings about the weaving techniques in 1969 in my publication for handweavers, *The Looming Arts*. We were soon out of print on all the issues and the idea of a book germinated.

Though the language barrier was always a problem during my research days on the reservation, I soon found out that there were differences of opinion among the Navajo weavers regarding weaving details. There is no one absolute set of rules for weaving a Navajo rug.

In recent years there has been much interest in the primitive weaves. The young people, particularly, have shown great interest and have hiked across the country to enroll in our Navajo and Hopi weaving classes.

Navajo and Hopi weaving looks very simple to most people and yet there are a number of rules that must be adhered to if one is to do a good job. I do not mean to imply that Navajo rug weaving or Hopi weaving is beyond the average person's intelligence. It is not, but it does take a certain amount of instruction and research in order to do the techniques correctly.

To learn to weave from the Indian is difficult. They do not have a set of rules to give you. They do not tell you why they do something a certain way. They show you and you have to see and comprehend each minute detail if you are to learn correctly.

With this book I hope to clarify many of the finer points that have yet to be available in print. I will give you easy to follow directions with no steps ignored.

I think it should be mentioned that Navajo weaving today is changing like everything else. The rugs being woven now are quite often made of commercial yarns or if not that, commercially carded wool, spun by the Navajo weaver. It would not be uncommon for the rug to be woven of imported yarns as some weavers are purchasing these in local yarn shops and re-spinning them to suit their need. Raising and shearing the sheep, carding, spinning and dyeing the wool is still being done but not to the extent as in the past. The younger weavers, and there aren't many, are looking for easier ways, the same as you and I.

The Hopi weaving section of this book will cover several types of fabrics. The Hopi men are the weavers. The setting up of the Hopi and Navajo looms is similar and the Hopi blanket weaving and Navajo rug weaving are much alike. However, the Hopi weavers do several other types of weaves that are not common to the Navajo.

To keep from duplicating weaving instructions in this book, I have referred back to previous chapters from the Hopi section to the Navajo section. This in no way implies that one type of weaving is more or less important than the other.

This is a book about weaving—Navajo and Hopi weaving. No history will be included.

I hope you will have great pleasure and enjoyment in learning the Indian weaves from this book. I certainly had fun writing it for you.

Mary Pendleton

NAVAJO TECHNIQUES

Contents

Introduction

Much has been written about how weaving is done by Navajos and others. This book, written by Mrs. Mary Pendleton, is the result of nearly twenty-seven years' weaving experience, the last five being directly involved with weaving similar to the way the Navajo women weave their rugs. Therefore, she is highly qualified to write this book that can be beneficial to whomever will be interested to read and learn.

Certainly, there is a great noted change which has taken place in rug weaving. According to the Navajo, the traditional story is of the mythical loom built by the Spider Man for Spider Woman with the cross poles made of sky and earth cords, warp sticks made of sun rays, a sun halo forming the batten and the comb made of white shell. There were four spindles representing the four directions: North—stick zigzag lightning with a whorl of jade; South—flash lightning with a whorl of turquoise; West—sheet lightning with an abalone whorl; and East—a rain streamer with a whorl of white shell.

As legend goes it was in October (*Ghaagii*), the month of black spiders, that the spiders came out of their dens and covered the ground before going into the world below. Therefore, weaving was taught during the month of October. Before the weaver touched her spindle she uttered a prayer and offered a sacrifice of precious stone, eagle feather and/or corn pollen so she could have good luck with her weaving. Unmarried girls were not permitted to weave. Today very few, if any, weavers still follow this traditional approach to weaving.

The years before the Long Walk were considered The Golden Age. Navajo women were producing Navajo rugs on a wholesale basis and practically all their trading was done with Navajo blankets. They were using many colors in weaving. Indigo dye was acquired from Mexico and red was acquired from Bayeta in flannel form. With blue and red, striped and intricate designs continued in popularity. In 1863, weaving came to an abrupt stop when Kit Carson started rounding up the Navajos and herding them into captivity at Fort Sumner, New Mexico. During their exile the production of Navajo blankets fell off to nothing.

The Navajos were in a condition of poverty. However, upon their return to their homeland, the United States Government induced some anglos to come into the Navajo country as licensed traders to trade with the Navajos.

One of them, J. Lorenzo Hubbell, came to Ganado, Arizona, about 1880 as an Indian trader. Mr. Hubbell encouraged the good weavers of Ganado to use red in their weaving. Because red was used in practically every rug woven at Ganado, it became known as Ganado Red. Weavers of Ganado still use red in their weaving today. Of course, there were other famous Indian traders, such as William Lippencott of Wide Ruins who was famous for the natural colored dye rugs woven in his area. George Bloomfield of Too Gray Hills and J. B. Moore of Crystal, New Mexico, were Indian traders who also promoted weaving in their areas. In this way a new era in weaving was introduced. These fine white men who came to the Navajo country saw the economic value of Navajo rugs and helped bring back into production the almost lost art of weaving and other crafts.

During the Second World War, many jobs were created for the Navajos. They worked in Ordinance Depots, along the railroads, in the copper mines and in defense industries all along the western coast of the United States. Jobs were numerous and Navajo men and women were employed with steady incomes. They sent money home to their families. As a result very few rugs were woven during this period.

Whoever reads this inclusive and excellent book will, I am sure, catch the spirit and find the inspiration that comes from the valuable information that is contained in it. It is very educational, not only to the person who may read for interest, but also for the Navajo women weavers.

Mrs. Mary Pendleton, known to me, can perform such weaving techniques as twill and double-faced rug weaving. In this book, she demonstrates her exceptional talents and omits no information. It is complete and thorough. I am sure that the information contained in this book may be more than some of the Navajo women may know.

Howard W. Gorman
Ganado, Arizona

Member of Navajo Tribal Council twenty-eight years

Member Board of Regents, Navajo Community College

Member Governor's Justice Planning Advisory Board

President Arizona Stabilization Commission for Apache County

Chairman Police Committee Navajo Tribe

Chairman Navajo Tribal Fair Commission

Howard Gorman, Navajo

How to Build Your Navajo Loom, Tools and Warping Frame

The Navajo works with very primitive tools. They must be constructed of what she has available. Many Navajos are still located in very remote areas on the reservation and even those who are not are still inclined to construct their tools and weave as their ancestors did. The women of the Navajo tribe are the weavers. It is said that the men help the women build their looms and make their tools, but the Navajo weavers that we have had teaching for us were amused by this remark.

The loom we are showing you how to make is one that fits into today's small living quarters. It is for small projects. It can be knocked down very easily for storage when not in use. This loom frame is like one we manufacture and use in our classes. It serves very well. It can be placed on a table for use or it can be secured to something solid for more stability and ease in weaving.

You will notice in diagram N1 that the top and bottom extend forward from the side pieces of the frame thereby permitting you to maneuver your battens and weaving tools without hindrance.

If you are interested in a large, heavy loom frame, refer to photo N1. One like this is being used at the boarding school in Chinle. You will have to decide how large a loom is most practical for you and your allotted space.

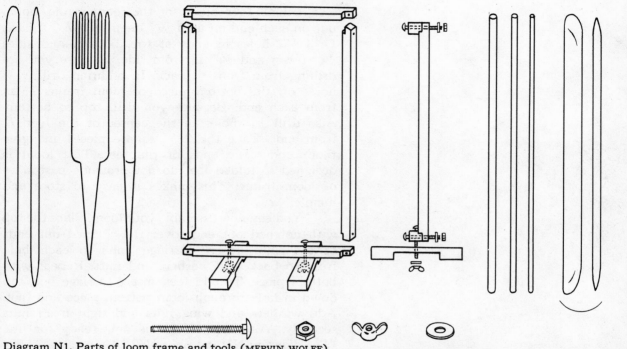

Diagram N1. Parts of loom frame and tools (MERVIN WOLFF)

The Loom Frame

A Navajo loom is not a difficult item to make. The loom can be very crude. You can probably do it with hand tools although power equipment would make the job easier and faster. The directions below are for a 31" x 44" loom, the suggested size for small projects.

Lumber Needed
2 pieces, 1½" x 1½" x 31" for top and
    bottom
2 pieces, 1½" x 1½" x 44" for sides
2 pieces, ¾" x 2½" x 14" for feet
4 pieces, ¾" x 2½" x 2½" for feet

Hardware Needed
six ¼" x 2½" carriage bolts
four ¼" hex nuts
two ¼" wing nuts
six ¼" flat steel washers

A good grade of white pine will do but you may wish to invest in hardwood. The battens, combs and dowels should be hardwood.

The larger the loom, the heavier the lumber should be so if you increase the size of this loom, use heavier materials. Also remember the loom frame must be a few inches wider and about 12" longer than the width and length of your project.

Since it is difficult to find a place to tie up a Navajo loom in today's homes, we are giving you information on making feet for your loom so it will be self-standing. The feet are removable in case you do not wish to use them.

On all four pieces of the loom frame, notch out on each end an area ¼" deep by 1½" square. Drill ¼"-holes in ends of top, bottom and sides ¾" down and ¾" in from side. Be sure you are drilling from front to back. In addition drill ¼"-holes on the bottom piece of loom frame 7" in from each end. Be sure you drill top to bottom. Also drill ¼"-holes in the center of the feet 7" from ends. Take the 2½"-square pieces and glue them under the ends of the feet. This loom is designed so folded feet do not protrude past sides of loom frame. This makes it easy to store and handle.

You can now assemble your loom. Place the top with notched out ends over the notched out ends of the sides. Insert carriage bolts in each hole front to back, add washers and nuts. Repeat with bottom piece. To add feet, insert carriage bolt top down in hole through loom bottom piece and foot. Add washers and wing nuts and tighten all nuts securely. Your loom frame is now ready for use. (See diagram N1 and photo N26.)

Additional Supplies Needed

(See diagram N1.)

Dowels—You will need two ⅜" dowels and three ¾" or 1" dowels all 26" long. They must be at least several inches longer than the width of your rug. When you get to the last part of your rug, it will be beneficial to have a ³⁄₁₆" dowel the same length as above.

You will often see the Navajo using broom handles for the heavier dowels and willow branches straightened and smoothed for the smaller dowels. These are often easier for her to come by than wooden dowels. I've seen some loom rods made from lengths of pipe.

The large dowels are used for mounting the warp on the loom. The smaller dowels are shed rods used to separate the warp threads during the weaving.

Battens—You will need at least three battens of different widths. The batten is the tool that keeps the warp threads separated while you put in the weft. I would suggest the widest one be 1½" wide, another about ¾" wide and one ⅜" wide. They should be made of hardwood and have a smooth surface so they do not wear the warp threads. The tight warp would soon wear grooves in a soft wooden batten. The battens should be about ¼" thick with one edge and both ends tapered. It is convenient to have them longer than the width of your weaving but on large projects there is a limit as to how long a batten you can handle. A good length for small projects is 24" or so long.

If you look closely at the battens the Navajo weavers use, you will see that they are slightly curved on one end. This, they feel, helps in inserting the batten into the shed. In my collection I have both straight and curved battens and one seems to work as well as another for me.

Comb—(sometimes called a fork). You will need several sizes of combs. This is a most important tool and is used to beat the weft in place. We give you directions for a size that works for most of your weaving but you will need to have one much smaller for the finishing of your rug. A table fork could be substituted for this smaller comb. The combs should be made out of hardwood. Be sure the end of the comb is quite pointed. This is helpful in weaving and unweaving. A good size comb to have is 9" long divided thus: 3" handle, 3½" center part and 2½" teeth. It is 1½" wide with six teeth and is ½" thick.

It seems to be the general opinion that a comb should be heavy but it is hard to define just how heavy. I have used a number of combs and I find that several are so heavy they pack the weft too tightly and are wearisome to hold. You need one heavy enough to do the job but it should be comfortable to use. Also consider that some shapes are more comfortable to hold than others.

It is not necessary to put a finish on your loom or tools unless you prefer it that way. It is best that the larger dowels not be too smooth. The cords stay put better if they aren't. As you work with the combs and battens, they will develop a smooth surface from the constant handling and contact with the wool yarns.

Miscellaneous Tools and Supplies

• Several bag or pack needles. On the reservation they are called sack needles. This is a heavy curved needle flattened at the pointed end. (See photo N62.) The Navajo may use instead an umbrella rib with a hole in the end.

• 26″ piece of wire similar to coat hanger wire

• Harness cord or heavy rope

• Heddle string, 8/4 carpet warp will do but a heavier yarn is better.

The Warping Frame
(See photo N13.)

Decide the length of rug you are going to weave. Then add 8″ or more and cut two pieces of 2″ x 4″ lumber to that length. Several inches in from each end of each piece hammer a heavy nail into the wood leaving a couple of inches protruding. The distance between these nails should be the length of your rug minus 2″. Cut two pieces of 1″ dowel at least 12″ longer than the width of your rug. If it is to be a wide rug, use a heavier dowel or piece of pipe.

With this completed, you now have all the necessary equipment for your weaving project.

If you do not wish to make your own equipment, please refer to Sources of Supplies in the Appendix.

Heavy Loom Frame
(See photo N1.)

This large, heavy loom frame is self-standing and does not have to be fastened to anything. You can have two projects going at once, one on the front and one on the back, or two weavers can work at the same time. It also is constructed so you can have projects longer than the height of the frame. The weaving can go under and around the lower dowel and fasten to another rod located in holes in center of outside frame.

With this loom, dowel rods on which warp is mounted must be longer than width of the loom

Photo N1. Large, heavy Navajo loom

so warp is held forward giving weaver free access to the shed. You can use this idea on any flat frame loom.

This heavy type of loom frame takes more room and is not as easy to take apart for storage.

About Yarns

Warp Yarn

It is very important that the warp yarn have certain qualities. It must be evenly and very tightly spun. It seems to me that we could say overspun to the point that when you relax the yarn it kinks up. There is tremendous tension on the warp yarn at all times and the pulling through of the weft and the beating of the comb puts constant wear on the warp. You do not want to be bothered with broken warp ends so select your warp yarn very carefully.

The better Navajo rugs are woven with a wool warp yarn. However, a good warp yarn is difficult to find. You can spin it yourself, or if you are not an experienced spinner, we suggest that you use 8/4 cotton carpet warp. This will serve the purpose for your first experiment with Navajo-type weaving. The cotton yarn has one disadvantage and that is it is more slippery than wool and the heddle stick doesn't stay put as well.

Another suggestion, if you are not a good spinner but can handle a spindle, respin commercial wool yarn. Take a three- or four-ply knitting worsted and respin it to make it stronger. It takes time but is not difficult to do. Another good yarn for respinning is the Canadian two-ply medium or three-ply wool.

To respin commercial yarn with a Navajo spindle, twirl the spindle away from you. Commercial yarn is a right twist and Navajo handspun yarn is a left twist.

I can't emphasize enough that the warp must be smooth and very tightly spun.

Weft Yarn

Your weft yarn is heavier than your warp. It should be softer spun so it can puff out between the warp ends and cover them. There are a few places that can supply you with Navajo handspun yarn or you can use commercial yarns or other types of handspun yarns. The qualifications of a good weft yarn are:

- Uniform in size
- Even twist
- Even dyeing

A thick and thin yarn or unevenly twisted yarn means you will have a lot of adjustment and filling in to do as you weave.

Commercial yarns that you can substitute for Navajo handspun yarns would be:

- Wool rug yarns
- Swedish Matt yarns
- Bulky size wool knitting yarns

If you plan to use your project for a rug, I wouldn't use the knitting yarns. The texture is too soft. They would be all right for handbags, pillow covers, etc. Please refer to Sources of Supplies in the Appendix.

Yarn for Twining

The wool yarn used for twining at both ends of your warp should be a two- or three-ply yarn medium to heavy depending on weight of other yarns used. It can be made from your weft yarn or it can be a commercial yarn. Since it becomes a part of the finished project, the color should be considered in the planning.

Yarn for Your Navajo Selvage Threads

This is usually the same yarn as used for the twining.

Preparing the Yarn Yourself

If you have decided to spin your own yarn, it will add to the pleasure of your project. For many years the Navajos depended on their flock of sheep for a source of food and income and some of the wool was used for their rugs. (See photo N2.)

To duplicate the Navajo's effort in yarn preparation, you will first need to acquire a fleece. This is not easy to do in some areas but usually you can find a 4-H member or a farmer who will sell a fleece. Otherwise check our Source of Supplies in the Appendix.

When you talk about strains of sheep on the reservation, the Rambouillet seems to be the one mentioned most but we will not take time to discuss the various types of sheep and which is the best wool producer for handspinning. Several of the books listed in the Reference List in the Appendix cover this subject.

Carding

To spin your yarn like the Navajo you need a pair of cards, usually size X or size 8 will do, a long spindle, usually about 32″ long, and some wool. Before you can spin the wool it must be carded. The purpose of carding is to straighten out the wool fibers so they lie parallel to each other. It also helps to eliminate the foreign matter.

Step 1—Take some wool and tease it by

Photo N2. Sheep herding (PHOTOGRAPH BY JOSEF MUENCH)

gently pulling it apart, opening up the locks and letting the foreign matter drop out. Continue teasing until fibers are loose and fluffy.

Step 2—Hold the bottom card in the left hand with handle and teeth of card pointing away from you. Your palm is up.

Step 3—With right hand, hook wool onto the teeth of the card. Distribute the wool as evenly as possible in a thin layer over the card. Too much wool on the card will result in poor separation of the fibers.

Step 4—With right hand, palm down, grasp the other card, called the top card, with teeth down and handle toward you.

Step 5—The carding: With left hand and bottom card resting on left knee, gently lay the heel (edge of card next to handle) of the top card over the heel of the bottom card and draw the top card toward you. Do not put so much pressure on the top card that the teeth of the cards mesh. They should barely touch. You will feel a combing action as the fibers are being transferred from the bottom

Photo N3. Grace Gorman demonstrating carding, Step 5

Photo N4. Carding, Step 6

Photo N5. Carding, Step 8

card to the top card. Continue with this action until no more fibers are being transferred. (See photo N3.)

Step 6—Transferring fibers from bottom card to top card: (See photo N4.) Without changing the way you are holding the cards, turn the top card over and place the toe (edge farthest from handle) of the bottom card over the heel of the top card and draw it down over the top card putting enough pressure on it so the teeth of the two cards mesh and the fibers left on the bottom card are transferred intact to the top card.

Step 7—Repeat Step 5.

Step 8—Transferring fibers from top card to bottom card: (See photo N5.) Turn top card over and place the toe of the top card over the heel of the bottom card and draw the bottom card up over the top card with teeth meshing. Now all the fibers are on the bottom card evenly spread out. Remember, the teeth of the cards barely touch when carding but they must mesh when you are transferring from one card to the other so you can lift the fibers without disturbing their order.

Step 9—Repeat Step 5 again. Continue carding, transferring fibers and carding until all fibers are evenly combed. End with fibers on bottom card.

Step 10—Removing fibers from cards: Repeat Step 6 very lightly *without* meshing teeth.

Step 11—Repeat Step 8 even more lightly.

Step 12—Repeat Steps 6 and 8 one more time. Fibers are now free of cards and you have a rectangular mass of fibers that should be light and airy.

Step 13—Place card with fibers in your lap and beginning at toe of card roll end of fiber mass toward handle and lift off card.

Step 14—Lightly roll this fiber mass between palms until elongated and fibers are evenly distributed. This is a rolag. Some spinners just lift the carded wool off the card and do not roll it.

Spinning the Yarn

First spin the wool fibers into roving, a soft thick yarn with very little twist. Then respin this roving into weft and if you wish it for warp, spin it again.

The Navajo uses a long spindle. She sits on the ground or on a low stool. The spindle is to her right with the top of the spindle shaft resting on the thumb of the right hand and all four fingers on top. The other end rests on the ground.

First Spinning

Step 1—Slip the end of the rolag over the end of spindle.

Step 2—Twirl the spindle *toward* you with a

fairly fast motion and let it slide back and forth between thumb and fingers. It tends to lean on your thigh while you spin.

Step 3—With left hand palm up, close the left thumb and index finger tightly around the fibers to be spun.

Step 4—While spindle is turning, the left hand holds the fibers so they are in line with the spindle shaft. As you twirl the spindle, a twist builds up between the end of the spindle and where you are holding the fibers with your left thumb and index finger. (See photo N6.)

Step 5—When you have enough twist (very little for this first spinning), stop twirling, hold the spindle and yarn with right hand and with left hand draw the fibers.

Step 6—As you draw the fibers, stretch and jerk the yarn. This slight jerking motion helps to let the twist advance evenly. Roving should be spun to about the size of your little finger. (See photo N7.)

Step 7—Now hold spindle vertically and roll the spun yarn onto the spindle shaft just above the whorl (the weight close to end of spindle shaft). (See photo N8.)

Step 8—Continue this twirl, stretch, jerk action until you have spun to the last few inches of your rolag.

Step 9—Overlap another rolag with the last few fibers of the first and continue. Do not let the yarn get too thick at the point where you overlap the two rolags. Be sure the fibers twist together to form a strong union.

Step 10—When the spun yarn gets as big as the whorl of spindle and is wound halfway up shaft, it's time to remove it. Unwind from the spindle into a soft ball. This is roving.

To Spin for Weft—To spin this roving for weft, take the end of the roving and slip it over the end of the spindle and repeat the above steps. Use the same motions as before but draw the roving out thinner. As you do this lumps of unspun fibers will probably appear. Take hold of yarn on either side of lump with thumb and index finger of both hands, roll between fingers to untwist it, draw out the fibers carefully and then relax your hold. These fibers should now twist into an even yarn.

To Spin for Warp—If you are spinning this yarn for warp, it will have to be drawn out much finer and spun very tightly. The Navajo sometimes spins it three times before she has the warp yarn she wants. However, my weaver friend at Many Farms prefers to spin her warp yarn in one spinning.

Setting the Twist—When yarn is spun as you

Photo N6. Ella Mae Neagle demonstrating spinning, Steps 1, 2, 3 and 4

Photo N7. Spinning, Steps 5 and 6

Photo N8. Spinning, Step 7

wish it, unwind it from the spindle. If it is for weft, you probably will want to skein it in preparation for dyeing. The Navajo winds her yarn under her foot and over her knee to make her skein. Tie the skein securely in several places. If you do not dye it, you should set the twist. Wet the yarn in lukewarm water—not hot—and hang it up to dry. Put a heavy weight on the skein to hold it under tension while drying. If you have spun for warp, you can do as some Navajo weavers do: wet fingers as you wind it into a hard ball.

Plying Yarn for Twining and Selvage Cord

Ply your handspun weft yarn for your twining and selvage cords. If your weft is too heavy, spin it finer.

Measure off two lengths of weft yarn each a little longer than the length of cord you need. With your Navajo spindle upsidedown fasten your double yarn to the shaft just below the whorl. With spindle lying on your right thigh short end to left, wrap the double yarn twice around the short end of the shaft clockwise and twirl the spindle away from you. This is opposite from the way you twirled the spindle while spinning the yarn. Twist it very tightly. When yarn is plied, wind it on shaft just below whorl. After plying, remove from spindle but hang onto the ends so you do not release the twist. Wet the yarn and stretch it around something to dry. Tie ends securely. When dry the twist will be set and the plied yarn ready to use.

Alternate Method—One of my friends on the reservation does the following: She spins her yarn very fine and tight. Then she chains it by making a loop in one end, reaches through this loop and draws another loop through, reaches through this loop and draws a loop through, etc. The loops are about 4″ long. Then she spins this chained yarn tighter on the short end of her spindle. This makes a three-ply yarn for twining and selvage cords.

Dyeing Your Handspun Yarn

Dyeing yarn can be very exciting. It gets you out of doors, it makes you aware of growing things and there is always that excitement of wondering what color will come out of the dye pot.

Here again dyeing could fill an entire book so we will just give you some information that will help you get started in dyeing your own yarns, and if you wish to get more technical about it, refer to some of the references listed in the Appendix.

Choose something handy from your garden or yard: apricot leaves, sagebrush, marigold blossoms, sunflower blossoms, walnut hulls, leaves or bark. Almost anything will make a dye.

Materials Needed:
5-gallon granite container, not chipped
Enough native material to fill container
1 pound wool yarn
Water
3 oz. alum
1 oz. cream of tartar
Cheesecloth
Long-handled wooden spoon or smooth stick
Gas or electric burner, open fire

First gather your native materials and cut them up into pieces small enough to go into the 5-gallon granite container. Have enough to fill it. Cover the native materials with water and boil for one hour or more. Remove the materials and strain the liquid through cheesecloth or similar material. Rinse out the container and pour in about 4 to 4½ gallons of the strained liquid dye.

An easy, fast way to dye yarn is to put the mordant into the dye bath instead of mordanting the wool first. The mordant makes the wool receptive to the dye.

Dissolve first and add to the dye bath 3 ounces alum and 1 ounce cream of tartar. Wash 1 pound of wool yarn thoroughly and drop it into the dye bath. If you are starting with clean yarn, be sure to wet it thoroughly before dropping it into the dye bath.

Bring the temperature up to simmer. The yarn will tend to float so keep pushing it under with a wooden spoon or wood stick so the dye will take evenly. Do not agitate or you will felt the yarn. It's just a matter of keeping the yarn submerged during the boiling time.

Simmer for about an hour. Let cool a little. Rinse the wool yarn in the same temperature water as the dye bath from which it was just removed. Continue to rinse until the rinse water is clear. Do not agitate while rinsing. Just squeeze the yarn gently enough to squeeze out excess water and hang up to dry.

Dyeing can be an endless occupation since there are so many types of plants to try.

About Design

Many Navajo rugs begin and end with a group of horizontal stripes. The more intricate patterning of the rug begins and ends several inches in from the ends. One weaver told me she does her designing this way because it is much easier to end the rug in a plain stripe area. We suggest you design your rug with this in mind.

You will see some rugs with an intricate pattern beginning immediately after the first four rows of weaving. In doing a rug like this, the weaver will weave about four or five inches of the intricate pattern or up to an area of pattern that is less complicated and then remove the rug from the loom frame, turn it upsidedown and put it back in the frame. She begins the rug again at the unwoven end. In this way when the two woven areas meet, it is easier to finish the rug because the tight weaving is done in a less complicated area. Please don't try this on your first project, however,

If you wish to follow exactly the sample rug shown, please do, but I would like to suggest that it would be more interesting for you to make your own design. In fact you may not want to make a rug. You may wish to make fabric for a handbag, pillow cover or table runner but whatever you decide to make, keep the design simple. Begin and end with horizontal stripes, then go to vertical lines and then into diamond shapes with diagonal lines. This will be the sequence of the instruction. Plan to use three colors. The colors in the sample are dark grey, light brown and white.

For those of you who decide to follow my design, I hope it is intricate enough to be challenging but simple enough not to be discouraging. If you wish to simplify it, eliminate some of the smaller design areas. (See diagrams N2 and N3.)

The Navajo weaver usually does not work out her design on paper first. She has an idea in her head and carries it out adjusting as she goes. I suggest you lay out your design on paper since this is your first attempt. Use a graph paper with ten squares to the inch. Let each square equal three or four warp ends so your paper need not be so large.

Before attempting your design, please read Selecting the Technique, which follows here. Also acquaint yourself with the design we will be using for our sample rug.

Selecting the Technique
Turned Lock or Interlock

There are two techniques used in forming vertical stripes in Navajo rugs. I call them the turned lock and the interlock methods. There seem to be differences of opinion as to which of these techniques should be used. In some rugs you find both represented.

My Navajo instructors prefer to teach the turned lock method first. This method seems to be easier for people to learn. In talking with the husband of a weaver at Ganado (his wife couldn't speak English), I learned that his wife used the interlock method on the long vertical lines of her

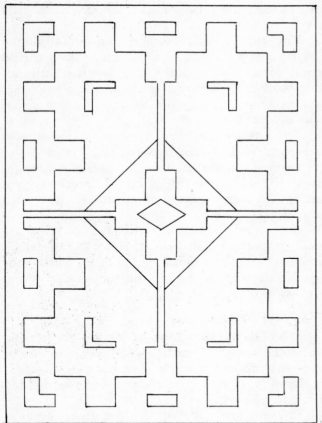

Diagram N2. Design used in sample rug

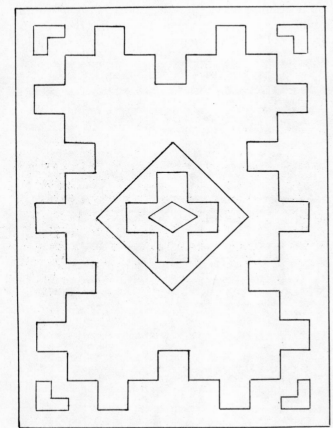

Diagram N3. Sample rug design simplified

Photo N9. Detail of Lower left, turned lock
method
Detail of Upper right, interlock
method

rugs but used the turned lock method on the short lines.

The turned lock method denotes adjoining wefts reversing direction on the same warp thread thereby forming a vertical line. This gives an interesting toothed or serrated effect and is a smoother joining though possibly not as strong a joining as in the interlock method.

The interlock method denotes the wefts locking around each other between warp threads to form vertical lines. Some feel that this is a stronger joining. However, at the point of interlocking a ridge develops and it is not as smooth as the turned lock method.

Both methods will be detailed as they are equally important. (See photo N9.) Decide which method you want to do before you wind your warp. If interlocking, we recommend an even number of warp ends.

Diagonal Lines

Most Navajo rugs have some kind of diamond shape represented. Diamonds can be flat, square or elongated with either straight or stepped edges. It just depends on how you want it and the method you use to weave it.

The diagonal line of the flat diamond is a smooth edge. It is formed by adjoining wefts turning on adjoining warp threads. There is a very small hole where the wefts reverse direction. (See photos N10 and N11.) The weight of your weft has a lot

Photo N10. Rug with flat diamond design, woven by Ella Mae Neagle

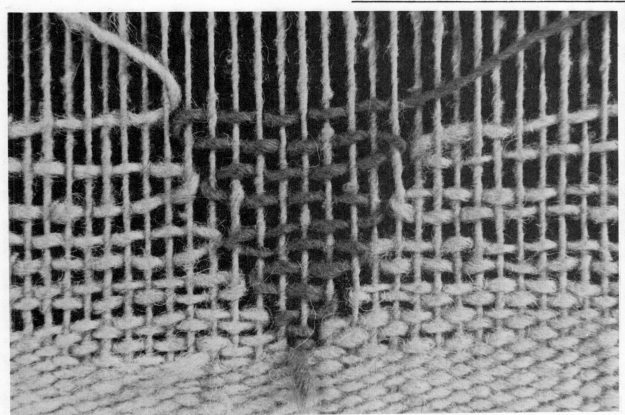

Photo N11. Detail of flat diamond. Adjoining wefts turn on adjoining warp threads.

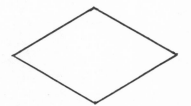

Flat diamond

to do with how flat your diamond will be.

The square diamond can be formed by short vertical lines advancing right and left to give a stepped edge. (See photo N12.) You can use either the turned lock or the interlock method of weaving.

The elongated diamond is achieved by weaving more rows before advancing right and left no matter what technique is used. (See diagram N4.)

Now with the preceding information in mind, you should be able to complete your design details.

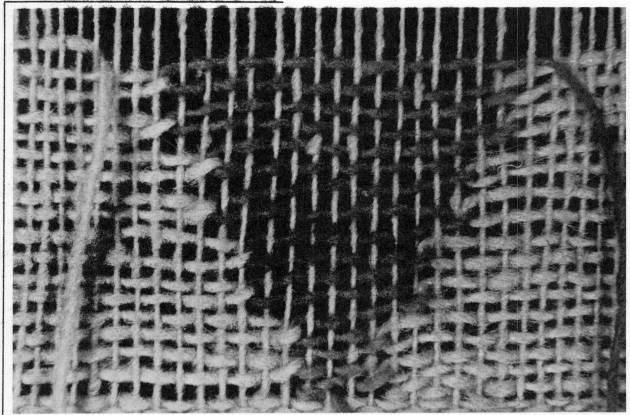

Photo N12. Detail of square diamond with stepped edge woven interlock technique.

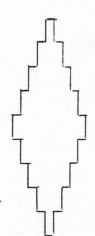

Square diamond with stepped edge

Diagram N4.

Square diamond with stepped edge can also be woven turned lock method to give serrated edge.

Elongated diamond can be woven either turned lock or interlock method.

Selecting Your Yarns and Planning the Setting

The size of your weft yarn determines how many warp threads per inch you should have. The warp must be so spaced that when the weft is beaten down there is room for it to puff out between the warp ends and cover them. The heavier the weft, the wider apart the warp is set. For the most part, the setting is usually about eight warp ends per inch. If a finer weft is used, the setting should be ten to twelve warp ends per inch. A very heavy weft would require a setting of six ends per inch.

My Selection of Yarns for Sample Rug

I selected a coarse weft yarn for the sample rug because I thought it would be easier to photograph and details of the weaving techniques would be more visible to you. In fact, the yarns are not the smoothest spun and have thick and thin places. The blending of the white and brown for the tan color is not even. This selection of less than perfect handspun yarns was intentional so I could show all the problems you might run into as well as the effect achieved when you work with such yarns. I figured that many of you would be using less than perfect yarns in your eagerness to get started. I find this attitude common among eager beginners.

The sample rug I have woven and photographed is not a perfect rug. It was not meant to be. I wanted it to be a typical rug showing all the various problems a weaver faces as she attempts her first piece of Navajo-type weaving. The photographs will help you visualize just what you should be doing or not doing.

Amount of Yarn Needed

Figuring the amount of warp yarn needed is a mathematical problem. Width in inches times number of warp ends per inch times length in inches divided by thirty-six will give you the yards you will need for warp.

The weft yarn is more difficult to determine because there are so many factors involved. The tighter you pack it down, the more you will need. The size of the weft and how tight or loose it is spun also makes a difference. I've weighed a number of pieces and they vary quite a bit. However, using medium weight handspun yarn on a warp set eight ends per inch (¼″ between pairs on warping frame), an average would be about one ounce of yarn to do thirty square inches of weaving.

To find the square inches of a project, multiply the width by the length. For instance, a saddle blanket 30″ x 30″ would be 900 square inches and would take about thirty ounces of weft yarn. Please keep in mind that this is only to be used as a guide; it's better to have too much yarn than too little.

Assembling Warping Frame

You can work either on the ground or on a table depending on how large you made your warping frame. In the photographs I am working on a table.

A Hopi friend of mine gave me the idea of putting a cloth underneath the warping frame so it does not slide around so easily. This really works and is worth remembering.

Set your two 2″ x 4″ pieces of wood on the table parallel to each other with the distance between them less than the length of your dowels. Place one dowel across the wood behind the nails at one end and repeat for other end. Tie dowels to 2″ x 4″'s very securely at each nail. Adjust frame so it is square. (See photo N13.)

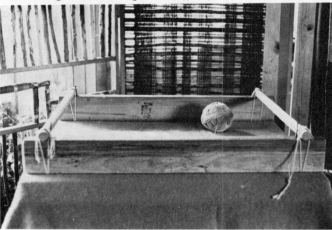

Winding the Warp

The Navajo weaver judges the distance by eye alone but you will want to mark your dowels at ¼″ intervals for a warp set eight ends per inch.*

Each mark represents one warp loop or two warp ends and if you want an even number of warp ends, you will need one extra mark on the dowel on which you begin the winding. If you want an uneven number of warp ends, you will need the same number of marks on each dowel. For example: To wind 100 warp ends (even number), you will have fifty-one marks on first dowel and fifty marks on the second dowel. To wind ninety-nine warp ends (uneven number) you will have fifty marks on each dowel. Our sample warp has 153 ends or seventy-seven marks on each dowel. (See photo N14.)

*The dowel marking for a twelve per inch warp would be every ⅙″ and for a six per inch warp every ⅓″.

Photo N13. Warping frame assembled and ready to use.

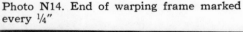
Photo N14. End of warping frame marked every ¼″

After you have marked both dowels, check to be sure the first marks on each dowel line up with each other. Standing with marked dowels on your right and left tie your warp at the first mark farthest from you on left dowel. Tie with a loose loop that you can untie later on. (See photo N15.) Now take your ball of yarn over and under the other dowel. Place the yarn on the first mark, pull tight, but not too tight, hold the tension. Now take the ball of yarn over and under the first dowel, place on mark, pull tight, hold tension. Repeat. You are actually winding a figure eight with the yarn crossing at mid-point between dowels. Continue winding in this manner, working toward you until you have the number of ends wound that you need for your warp. Break yarn and tie with loose loops as in beginning. (See photo N16.)

The Navajo weaver doesn't figure in advance and count the warp ends as we do. She winds what she thinks will give the right width judging by eye alone and fastens the yarn but does not break it. Then after she twines and spaces out the warp accurately, she adds or subtracts warp ends to give the width she wishes. Then she breaks off the yarn and ties it.

While you are winding your warp, it is most important that you do not bump or move your frame and cause it to become out of square. At all times the 2″ x 4″ pieces of wood and dowels must stay at right angles with each other. If you gradually keep pulling the tension of your warp tighter and tighter it will cause the frame to move out of shape.

Every so often check the cross. Bend down and sight across the warp. Look above and below. If a warp end is straight across from one dowel to the other and out of line with the rest of the warp, unwind to error and correct. The first and last warp ends will always be out of line so don't get panicky when you discover this.

To summarize:
• DO keep tension taut and even.
• DO keep warp loops ¼″ apart on marks.
• DO check often to see that your cross is made correctly.
• DON'T pull some warps tighter than others.
• DON'T bump warping frame and get it out of square.

Twining to Space the Warp

You now have all your warp threads wound and the loops at beginning and end are loose so they can be slipped off the dowels easily. You have double checked to see that you have wound the right number of warp ends. To keep the warp ends

Photo N15. Warp tied to warping frame with loose loop and knot that can be untied later

Photo N16. Warp partially wound on warping frame

spaced evenly, twine a cord between the warp ends as follows:

Take a two- or three-ply wool yarn—either a commercial yarn or the yarn you fashioned from your own handspun wool. This twining cord becomes a part of your rug so be sure the color fits into your color scheme. Measure off two pieces twice the width of the rug plus about 40". Take one length and double it. Tie a large loop, about 10", at the doubled end. Beginning at the left side, take one end of this twining cord under first warp loop or through loose loop, whichever it is. Pull through so loop knot is touching first warp. Drop this twining cord and pick up cord two from below. Take cord two under second warp loop and pull through. Drop and pick up cord one from below and take under third warp loop. Each time you pick up a cord from below you are crossing the two ends once between the warp loops as they lay on the dowel. Be sure you keep the same tension on each twining cord and be sure the twining cord lies parallel with the dowel. (See photo N17.) Continue across warp in this manner. At last warp thread, tie the two ends of twining cord in same knot as at beginning. Repeat this twining on other end of warp. It is important that you twine each end with same tension so both ends of rug will be equal in width.

To summarize:
• Tension of twining must be even.
• There must be one twist between each warp pair. If you miss one, you must correct it.
• When twining is complete, both warp ends must be same width.

Alternate Method—You can use three cords for the twining if you want something a little special. Use the same rules as for two cords, only add one step. Take cord one under the first warp loop, take cord two under the second warp loop, take cord three under the third warp loop. Pick up cord one from under cords two and three and take it under fourth warp loop. Pick up cord two from under cords three and one and take it under fifth warp loop. Pick up cord three from under cords one and two and take it under sixth warp loop. Continue in this manner across warp.

If you use a triple cord for twining, you should use a triple cord for the selvage threads.

Securing the Cross

To preserve the cross in the middle of the warp, take a length of yarn more than twice the width of the warp and insert one end in same opening of warp as dowel on left and insert the other end in same opening of warp as dowel on right.

Photo N17. Twining to space warp ends

Bring two ends together on same side of warp. Be sure this cross tie catches the two end warp threads. They will be lying slightly out of line and can easily be missed. Knot ends. The cross is now secured. (See photo N18.)

Removing Warp from Frame

I am going to give you two methods of removing warp from warping frame and binding warp to rods of loom frame. Method Number One is the way Navajos have been doing it for years and many still do. Method Number Two is being taught at Navajo College.

Method Number One—We are ready to remove the warp from the warping frame. Loosen one dowel, push the warp threads together and tie the ends of the twining cord in a loose knot that can be untied later. (See photo N19.) Repeat on other end. Slip warp off dowels.

It looks like a mess, doesn't it? But it isn't really. Handle it carefully and it will straighten out at the right time. Don't let it roll back or twist around itself.

Binding Warp to the Loom Rods, Method Number One—You now need the dowel rods of your loom and a strong, heavy, string yarn; 8/4 cotton carpet warp doubled will do but something heavier would be better.

Lay your warp out on the table and untie one twining cord very carefully. Don't let go of it and

Photo N18. A string tie secures the cross

Photo N19. Removing warp from frame, Method Number One

Photo N20. Fastening warp to loom rod, Method Number One

let it roll up and wrap around itself. Put a weight on one end if necessary to hold it down and lay the other end of the twining cord parallel to one of your loom dowel rods. Take the 10″ loop of the twining cord, split it and tie it securely to the loom dowel rod. Wrap it around several times before you tie knot. Stretch twining out parallel to dowel and repeat fastening on other end. Be sure the warp is centered on rod. (See photo N20.) Now take a piece of heavy binding cord (about 1″ per warp end plus about 60″ if you bind between every pair of warps. You can always tie on if you run out) and fasten to dowel on left side. Wrap around rod several times over knot of twining cord. Separate the first warp thread or warp pair, whichever it is, and wrap the binding cord around the dowel, over the twining in between warp pairs. Pull tight. (See photo N21.)

Photo N21. Binding warp to loom rod, Method Number One. The right hand is holding the binding cord and the left hand is separating the warp loops.

The Navajo weaver will bind between each warp pair for three or four pairs and then in between every two pairs until she reaches the other side where she ends as she began. However, I recommend that you bind in between every warp pair for this first project. All the tension of the warp when it is stretched in the frame pulls against this cord so IT IS VERY IMPORTANT THAT YOU PULL THIS CORD AS TIGHT AS POSSIBLE. Keep twining cord parallel with dowel rod. It is easy to pick up one warp of one pair and a warp of the adjoining pair and think they are one pair so guard against this. Fasten securely on right side. Repeat this procedure on other end of warp. Hold loom dowel rods together to check width. Both ends should be the same. (See photo N22.)

You now have your warp fastened between two dowel rods. This is what is called "the Navajo Movable Loom" and it is now ready to be mounted in the loom frame.

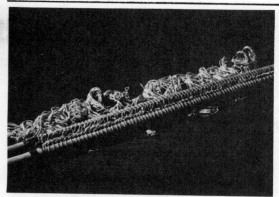

Photo N22. Verify that each end of warp is stretched to same width on rods.

To summarize:
• When you untie twining cord, guard against warp rolling up and twisting around itself.
• The binding must be very tight.
• Be sure you are getting the right warps in each pair.

Method Number Two—After you have finished twining both ends, take one of your loom rods and lay it parallel to end of warping frame next to twining cord. Tie ends of twining cord to loom rod. Thread a bag needle with your binding cord and tie a slip knot in long end. Slip this end loop over loom dowel rod. Wrap binding cord around rod several times before starting the binding. Take point of needle down *between* twining cord and warping frame dowel, around loom rod and pull tight. Be sure point of needle goes between pairs of warp threads and that it does not damage any warp yarns and weaken them. Continue across warp, binding between each warp pair and fasten securely at other side. Repeat on other end of warp. (See photo N23.)

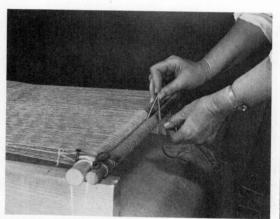

Photo N23. Binding warp to loom rod, Method Number Two

Now untie the loose loops that hold the first and last warp threads and tie to loom rod. Adjust tension like other warp. By fastening these warp ends this way, you do not have double warp loops on edge of rug. Remove warp from warping frame by untying at corners.

This method of fastening the warp to the loom rods is much faster than Method Number One. It's a more recent procedure but is being used quite widely on the reservation by the new weavers.

To summarize:
• Lay loom rod parallel to warping frame rod.
• Bind with bag needle very tightly.
• Be sure needle point goes between warp pairs.
• Guard against damaging warp with needle point.

Mounting Warp in Loom Frame

You need your third loom rod and a heavy

Photo N24. Inserting tie cords for mounting warp in loom frame. Tie cord goes *between* the twining cord and loom rod.

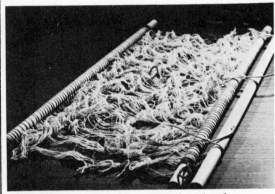

Photo N25. Adding third loom dowel rod

cord or rope about 7 yards long depending on length of warp and size of loom frame. You should decide which end of your warp will be the top. If you have any difference at all put the widest width on top.

Cut six 12″ lengths of your heavy cord, three for the bottom and three for the top. Insert one 12″ cord a few inches from each edge of warp and one in the middle. This cord goes *between* the twining cord and the dowel, *not* over the top of the twining cord. (See photo N24.) If you have bound the warp to the loom dowel rod tightly as you should have, you may have some difficulty in getting this heavy cord in place. A crochet hook can be used to draw cord through. Repeat on bottom.

With the six cords in place, lay the third loom rod parallel to the dowel at top of warp and tie, leaving 1″ of space between the two rods. (See photo N25.) I use a square knot. One of my Navajo instructors uses rawhide lengths to tie these two dowels together and she puts a twist between.

Standing in front of your loom frame fasten an end of your heavy cord on the left. Fasten securely by wrapping around the frame and over the end of the cord several times. Holding the third loom rod with warp attached, bring end of heavy cord through 1″ space between second and third loom rods, over top of frame, and repeat four or five times or more depending on the width of your rug. The path of this heavy cord is always around and encircling the loom rod and top of loom frame and never between the two.

Fasten cord to top of loom frame on right. To fasten easily, wrap cord around loom frame several times, then holding cord near frame, double end back around in opposite direction. You now have a loop and an end to tie with. Adjust so the bottom loom rod is just touching the bottom of the loom frame. (See photo N26.)

Tie bottom loom rod to bottom of loom frame very tightly. Here again a square knot is the best. Be sure ties are the same tension so when warp is tightened the bottom rod remains parallel to the bottom of loom frame.

With bottom fastened, tighten warp (see Tensioning of Warp, page 40), then check the following: Space between warp and sides of loom frame should be the same at top and bottom. Each edge should measure the same from top to bottom. It's easy to put more tension on one side than the other so check this carefully.

To summarize:

• Heavy cord goes *between* twining cord and dowel.

Photo N26. Mounting warp in loom frame

- Edge warp threads must be parallel to sides of loom frame. Measure for exactness.
- Bottom loom rod must be parallel to bottom of loom frame.

Warp must be stretched very tight.

Alternate Method of Mounting Warp in Frame

One of our Navajo instructors mounts her warp a little differently. She ties the bottom of the warp to the bottom of the frame first and then laces the top dowel to the loom frame and tightens it up. After working with the students in my studio, I find it much simpler for most people to hang the warp loosely in the frame first and then tighten as in the first method we described.

Tensioning of Warp

There is a knack to tightening the warp for the right tension. Proceed as follows:

Reaching between the top of loom frame and rod number three, grasp the cord with your left hand and push away from you while the right hand is grasping the extension of this cord in front and pulling down. Without releasing tension take the front cord in your left hand and with right hand grasp the next front cord. The left hand moves to the next back cord. By pushing the back cords and pulling down on the front cords you work your way across carrying the slack to the edge where you can untie and adjust tension. Repeat this several times until you have a good tight warp. You may need to use opposite hands, depending on whether you are taking the slack to the right or left side.

Marking the Centers of Your Warp

At this point it would be the best time to count off your warp and mark the centers. If you have an even number of warp ends, find the two center ones and encircle them with a piece of yarn and push it to the top. If you have an odd number just mark the center thread.

When you have your warp tightened ready to weave, measure to find the center from top to bottom and mark the center warp thread or threads at this point. Depending on your design you may wish to mark off several other points. Having your warp marked helps when you are doing pattern weaving.

Inserting the Shed Sticks into Warp

Take one of your shed sticks, ⅜″ dowel, and put it into the warp replacing the top half of your cross tie. An easy way to do this is to pull a few inches of the tie toward you to make an opening for the stick. (See photo N27.) Insert a batten in

the bottom half of the cross replacing the lower portion of the cross tie. I would suggest that you do not remove the cross tie yet.

Making Heddles

Take the end of your heddle cord (leave it attached to your ball or tube as you don't know just how much you will need) into shed made by batten from right to left. At the end of this heddle cord tie a loop about 2″ long. Double this loop back (like in a snitch knot) and put over right end of second shed stick. (See diagram N5.) The right end of this shed stick is held to the left of the warp in front of the batten. This shed stick is held like a pencil in your left hand and the index finger gauges the length of heddle; that is, the thickness of your index finger plus a little is usually about the right length for the heddle.

Reach between first and second warp ends on front side of batten and pull heddle string through. Twist once to the right and loop over end of shed stick. (See photo N28.) After you have looped the heddle string over the stick, reach to the right side of the warp and pull on the heddle string to adjust

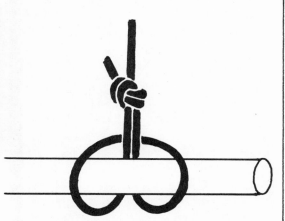

Diagram N5. Fasten heddle cord to shed stick by doubling a loop back like in a snitch knot or sling knot and inserting shed stick in opening. (MERVIN WOLFF)

Photo N28. Making the heddles

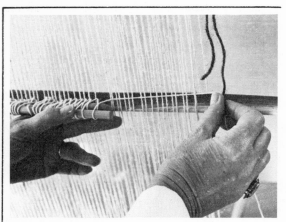

Photo N29. Adjusting length of heddle

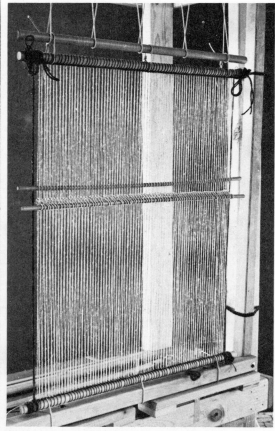

Photo N30. The Navajo loom ready to weave on with shed stick, heddle stick and selvage threads added.

the length of the heddle. (See photo N29.) The heddle length should be at least 1″ long. Be sure you keep the heddle length even. Continue until you have a heddle made around every warp end on front of batten.

As you tie heddles you have to move stick to the right. To do this easily, take hold of right end of stick with right hand and twist it back and forth as you pull it to the right. In this way, it will move through the heddles without disturbing their position. To finish, tie a loop as in beginning and slip over end of heddle stick. The two loops at either end should *not* be tight on stick.

When you are sure everything is correct, remove cross tie string.

To summarize:
• A heddle is made around every warp end on front of batten.
• All heddles must be at least 1″ long.
• All heddles must be the same length.
• End loops of heddle string must *not* be tight around heddle stick.

Adding the Selvage Threads

Most Navajo rugs have an edge thread that is both useful and decorative. It adds strength to the rug as well as being an integral part of the design. Using either commercial yarn or your handspun plied yarn, cut two pieces twice the length of your rug plus about 24″. Tie the loop end to bottom dowel next to edge of warp. Rub the two strands between your palms to twist the yarns, take them behind the shed sticks and tie to dowel number two with a tension that almost matches the warp. Repeat on other side. Twist the yarns in the opposite direction to what you plan to twist in the weaving. In this way you won't have to release the built up twist so often.

One of my Navajo instructors says she always wets her selvage yarns and shrinks them before using. (See photo N30.)

Things to Know before You Start to Weave

• Making the Sheds
• How to Use your Batten
• How to Use your Comb
• Warp and Weft Tension
• How to Break Weft Yarn
• How to Splice Weft Yarn
• How to Fill Low Places to Keep Weaving Line Even
• The Navajo Selvage

Making the Sheds

As soon as you have your heddles made, you can make the two sheds necessary to weave.

Bring the top shed stick down on top of the heddle stick. The warp threads will separate below the sticks. This is called the stick shed. (See photo N31.) Now push the shed stick to top of warp and with heddle stick in a middle of the warp position grasp it palm down with your left hand and pull it forward. The shed thus created is called the pull shed. (See photo N32.) In actuality you are bringing every other warp thread forward with the stick shed and the alternate warp threads forward with the pull shed.

If you are using a wool warp, the warp ends may stick together. It pays to brush the back of your finger tips across the warp just before making the shed to loosen any sticky threads. This is particularly necessary for the pull shed.

How to Use Your Batten

The batten is either in your hand or in the shed most of the time. You don't want to put your tools down any more than is necessary. Establish good weaving practices right from the beginning.

The batten is inserted into the shed with the longest edge up, then turned horizontally to spread the warp and make the shed larger, ready to receive the weft yarn. The longest edge is turned to the front. Use both hands to turn the batten.

To remove the batten turn it vertically again with long edge back on top and, with right hand palm up, grasp the batten with thumb and index finger. Pull out part way, move hand toward center of batten and pull all the way out. The bottom edge of batten will be resting on the third finger and the fourth and fifth fingers will be holding your comb. The batten is now in the right position for inserting into next shed. (See photo N33.)

Photo N33. Correct way to hold batten and comb

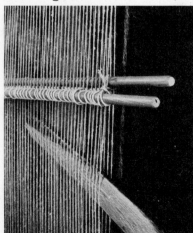

Photo N31. Making the stick shed

Photo N32. Making the pull shed

How to Use Your Comb

The comb is used to beat your weft into place. The pointed end of the handle is used to bubble, to lift wefts in correcting tension and to unweave. In the last part of the weaving it can be used to push wefts into place. (See photos N34, N65, N77.)

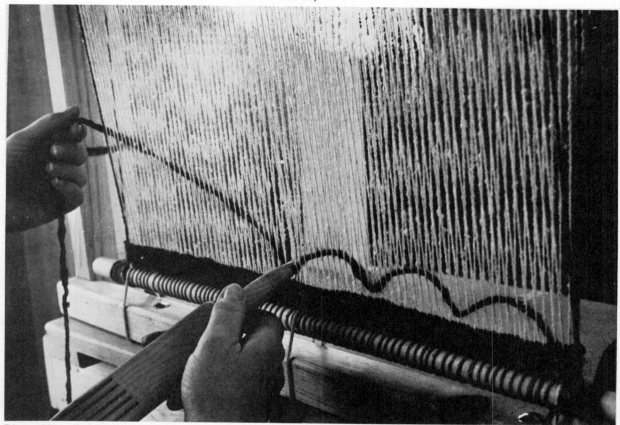

Photo N34. Bubbling the weft using point of comb—weft at first three warps placed with comb before bubbling.

Photo N35. Correct way to hold comb—beating from bound end of weft.

The comb should be in your hand at all times along with the batten. (See photo N33.) While you are making sheds, inserting batten and splitting selvage yarns over batten, the comb is held down out of the way. To lay your comb down and pick it up every time is wasted motion and the sign of a novice weaver.

When you are beating weft into place, hold the comb as shown in photo N35. The hammer motion used in beating the weft into place comes from a loose wrist movement. It is not a pressing motion. The action must be firm and strong.

Not until you are finishing the rug will you change the action of the comb. When the weaving space becomes small and the warp very tight during the last few inches of weaving, you do not have room to beat. The motion of the comb then becomes a pressing into place action. By this time you will have switched to a smaller comb. Press first with one edge of the comb as you gradually lower it down to meet the weaving. (See photos N58 and N59.)

Warp and Weft Tension

Navajo rug weaving is a type of tapestry weave in which the weft yarn must completely cover the warp. It is a plain weave in that alternate warp threads are brought forward on alternate rows of weaving.

Warp tension has but one rule. It should be very tight. Many of your problems can be avoided if you remember this. Your warp yarn may stretch as you weave and beat so keep adjusting tension. If the warp is not tight, it will feel spongy when you beat. Too loose a tension in the warp can cause problems such as:

- Weft does not beat down as easily
- Warp ends separate more readily where colors join
- Side edges bulge out
- Side edges draw in
- Batten keeps turning vertically in shed

Handling the weft yarn is very important and you must understand the finer points before beginning your project. The weft should be laid in the shed diagonally and beaten down from the bound end toward the free end. There must be enough looseness so it can puff out between the warp yarns and cover them. If you are weaving all the way across with one weft, with the point of your comb at intervals press the weft down to the weaving, forming scallops or bubbles. This draws extra yarn into the shed. We call this bubbling. (See photos N34 and N35.) The Navajo weaver does not bubble her weft but we suggest you start this way until you get the feel of it.

I would suggest the bubbles to be about 3″ long and about ¾″ to 1″ at peak from weaving. This will vary with size and twist of yarn. A little experimentation will tell you when you have the right amount of weft in the shed.

When you are weaving in the pattern areas where the individual wefts may cover only a few inches at a time, you may not want to use the bubbling method of forming scallops. The Navajo weaves only a few inches through the shed at a time and then beats this in place. She holds the end of weft with her left hand putting *little or no* tension on it and beats with her right hand beginning at the bound end of the weft. As the comb beats the weft down, the right amount of weft is drawn into the shed.

If you pull your weft too tight, the following things will happen:

• The entire width will draw in.

• The warp threads will show through the weft.

• The warp threads will draw closer together in some areas.

• Too much space will develop between warp threads at vertical color lines.

By the same token you can get too much weft in the shed. If you do, the following will happen:

• Small loops will appear on both front and back surfaces.

• The outside edge will be forced out.

• If you are careless and weave an area very tight and then loosen up for a time, rippled areas will result.

The right tension is very important so be always on guard. Don't be afraid to unweave and correct.

How to Break Weft Yarn

Your first thought may be, what an unnecessary instruction. However, it's the attention to little things that make the whole successful.

You will be working with short lengths of weft so you will have to break the yarn often. To do this, untwist the yarn and pull apart. The ends of the weft will have fewer fibers and will be tapered. Cut yarn gives you blunt ends that are difficult to hide.

How to Splice Weft Yarn

If you have broken the weft yarn as directed, the ends of your weft will be tapered. When you run out of one piece you just overlap one tapered end with the other for about 1″. The two tapered ends fit together to make an even splice. Never splice on edge of rug. Always splice an inch or so inside the edge. (See photo N36.)

Always end a weft yarn by pulling it apart and retwisting the fibers before you lay in shed. Overlap with the new yarn. Sometimes in my excitement of getting on with the pattern I forget to end the yarn and just let it hang and go on weaving. Later I have to cut this yarn. If you find yourself doing this, cut the yarn at an angle and as unevenly as you can so you don't have a blunt end showing.

Details of fastening in new colors will be given as they arise in the woven sample.

How to Fill Low Places to Keep Weaving Line Even

Several things can cause low places in your weaving:

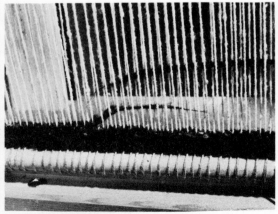
Photo N36. Splicing weft yarn

• Unevenly spun yarn

• Uneven twist in yarn—where it's twisted the least it's softer and packs down more than the harder twisted areas.

• Uneven tension in the warp

• Warp yarns not evenly spaced—weft packs down more where warp is more open.

The weaving line must be kept even or your stripes and pattern areas will not be lined up with the beginning of your project. The minute you discover a low place developing, fix it. If the low area covers just a short distance, you can do it with your fingers without using the batten to change sheds.

Let's say you are weaving right to left when you discover a low area.

Step 1—Bring weft yarn to top of warp on left of low area.

Step 2—Turn batten vertically in shed.

Step 3—Over the low area pick up opposite shed with right index finger; that is, pick up the warps from the back of the batten. (See photo N37.)

Step 4—Using index and third fingers of left hand push weft left to right through this shed made by your right index finger.

Step 5—Keep these two fingers in the shed while the right hand pulls weft on through. Don't

Photo N37. Step 3—Pick up other shed in preparation for filling low place in weaving.

Photo N38. Step 5—Keep picked up shed open with fingers of left hand while pulling weft through shed.

Photo N39. Step 8—Weave right to left in original shed.

remove fingers too soon and drag the weft yarn through a closed, tight shed. (See photo N38.)

Step 6—Beat weft into place.

Step 7—Turn batten horizontally.

Step 8—Insert weft and weave right to left on across the warp. You have actually woven two more rows of weft over this low area filling it in. (See photo N39.)

If the low area is very minute, just wrap your weft once around one warp thread to fill. (See photo N40.)

If you discover that one side of your weaving is higher than the other, do this: When weaving toward the high side, do not weave all the way to the edge. Keep reversing your weft inside the edge and closer to center each time until the weaving height is the same on both sides. Always reverse on a different warp thread each time.

If you discover that both sides of the weaving are higher than the middle, do this: Don't weave out to either edge. Keep reversing the weft inside the edges and closer to the middle each time until center is level with edges.

Do keep small low areas corrected so large low areas won't develop.

The Navajo Selvage

There are several ways that the Navajo handles the weaving of the edge selvage threads. Three methods will be discussed. Method Number One is the one used most widely by the Navajo weavers.

Method Number One—The position of the edge warp yarn is the key. It tells you which selvage threads to split. The selvage is two threads. By split we mean to divide the two threads and bring one to the front of the batten and leave the other in back.

After you make your shed, split the selvage threads on the side that has the edge warp yarn on the *back* of the batten. If you have an *even* number of warp threads in your warp, you will split selvage threads first on one side on one row then on the other side on the next row. When not split, the selvage threads remain in back of the batten.

If you have an *odd* number of warp threads in your warp, you will find on one shed both edge warp yarns come to the *front* of the batten and on the other shed both edge warp yarns are in *back* of batten. When both edge warp ends are on the *back* of the batten, you split both right and left selvage threads. On the opposite shed do not split either selvage.

Each time you split the selvage threads, you bring the *same* one to the front of the batten. This is the one that is being woven at the time. After you have woven eight rows (four loops around selvage thread), you bring the other selvage thread to the front and weave it for eight rows. When you bring this new one to the front, it comes from the back, between the first warp thread and other selvage thread. You are actually twisting the two selvage threads. The twist should be made often enough so the skips on edge are not too long. As you weave, the twist of the selvage threads builds up and every so often you have to untie and release the twist.

With this method the selvage threads weave separately and not with the first warp thread. (See diagram N6.)

Method Number Two—Some weavers use a method that always puts the selvage thread with the outside warp thread. If you prefer this way, simply change the rule as follows: When the outside warp thread is on the *front* of the batten, you split the selvage threads. This causes them to weave together as a double thread.

Both methods are acceptable. It's a matter of personal preference.

Method Number Three—For a more decorative edge use a triple cord for the twining and the selvage. Use the same rules as for weaving with two selvage threads but add one step.

Use thread one for eight rows, then twist and use thread two for eight rows then twist and use

Photo N40. Fill very minute low areas by wrapping yarn around just one warp thread.

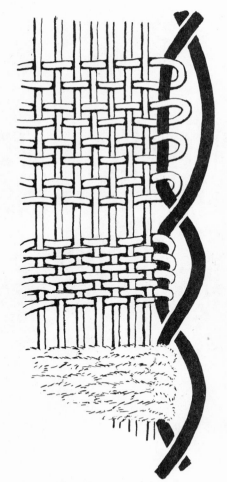

Diagram N6. Correct path of selvage threads Method One. (MERVIN WOLFF)

Photo N41. A selvage correctly woven using Method Number One.

Photo N42. Picked up shed for first row of weaving

thread three for eight rows, then back to thread one, etc. Depending on the weight of your weft, you may wish to weave less rows before you twist as each selvage thread floats for twice the amount of rows you weave on each thread.

Alternate Twist Direction—Not all weavers twist their selvage threads as we have stated above. Here are two other ways to twist:

1. Twist left to right on right side and right to left on left side bringing selvage thread from the outside *front to back* between first warp and other selvage thread putting twisted thread on *back* of batten.

2. Twist both sides in the *same* direction using either of the two twists mentioned above.

See photo N41 which shows how the selvage should look. Here I have just made the twist and I'm ready to weave with the alternate selvage thread.

Exception to above rules—When you are working your selvage threads with a one and one color arrangement of wefts, the rules given above do not produce a good edge. I have been unable to pin down my Navajo weavers with any set way but my own experimentation tells me the best way is as follows: Split the selvage threads for two succeeding rows and do not split for the next two succeeding rows.

Beginning the Weaving
The First Four Rows

The first and last four rows of the weaving are different from the regular weaving. The purpose of this is to cover the ends of the warp.

Step 1—Push your shed rods to top of warp as you do not use these now.

Step 2—With your batten pick up alternate pairs of warp threads across the bottom of the warp. If your first warp thread is a single end, then pick up this one and proceed with the pairs as they stand together. (See photo N42.) Do not include selvage threads. They will be in back of batten for these first four rows.

Step 3—Turn your batten horizontally.

Step 4—From right to left put your weft (I'm using dark grey) through opening made by batten. This is called the shed. You can either push the weft through the shed with your fingers or use a narrow stick shuttle.

Step 5—Pull the end of the weft to just inside the right edge to begin.

Step 6—Beat weft into place. Weft should be loose enough in shed to allow it to be beaten down between warp pairs.

Step 7—Turn batten vertically and remove.

Step 8—For the second row pick up opposite warp pairs.

Step 9—The third row is like the first.

Step 10—The fourth row is like the second.

After you weave the four rows your weft is on the right side. You are now ready to weave the regular way using the stick shed and the pull shed and including the selvage threads. We assume you are beginning with a solid stripe as suggested. Proceed as follows:

Regular Weaving

Step 1—Make your shed. We began with the stick shed.

Step 2—Insert batten always with long side up.

Step 3—Check to see if the outside warp threads are on the front or back of the batten.

Step 4—Where the outside warp thread is on the *back* of the batten, split the two selvage threads and put one of them on the *front* of the batten. *Do not stretch* this thread out over the batten end but pull the end of batten to the selvage thread so it will go over easily. On our sample both outside warp ends are on the front of batten so we do not split on this shed. Our warp has an odd number of warp ends. Adjust directions to suit your warp. (See Navajo Selvage for details, page 48.)

Step 5—Turn batten horizontally.

Step 6—Push weft through shed right to left.

Step 7—Holding the weft with your left hand with practically *no* tension on it, use the point of your comb to make your scallops or bubbles. (See photo N34.)

Step 8—Beat with comb beginning at the bound edge at right and work to left. (See photo N35.)

Here's a hint that we use in tapestry weaving to help keep edges straight and keep you from drawing in. When the weft is in the shed and just before you use the point of your comb to form the bubbles, use your comb to set the weft at the bound edge by pressing the weft into place over the first three warp threads, then do your bubbling with the point of the comb. (See photo N34.)

Step 9—Turn batten vertically with long end back on top.

Step 10—Remove from shed. If you don't turn your batten vertically before pulling it out, it will wear your warp threads.

Step 11—Make the pull shed and insert batten.

Step 12—Split the correct selvage threads and bring one to front of batten. Since I have an odd number of warp ends, I split selvage on both sides.

Step 13—Turn batten to horizontal position.

Step 14—Push weft through shed left to right.

Step 15—Bubble and beat.

Step 16—Turn batten vertically and remove.

You should not have laid your comb down even once but kept it in your hand turned down out of the way when not in actual use. (See photo N33.)

Continue the above until you have four weft turns around the selvage threads you have been bringing to front of batten. The next time you are to split the selvage threads, you will change and bring the opposite one forward thereby making the twist. (See Navajo Selvage for details, page 48.)

As you run out, splice your weft yarn an inch or more *away* from the edge of your rug. (See How to Splice Weft Yarn, page 46.) Continue until your horizontal stripe area is complete and you are ready to begin your pattern. My stripe area is 1⅛". Be sure you have no low areas and the weaving is even before you introduce new colors.

Do not begin your pattern until you have mastered horizontal stripes and selvage threads. Don't be afraid to take out and do over. Your rug may be twice-woven before you're through but that's part of the learning process.

Our sample rug will show two techniques of weaving—the turned lock and the interlock. I feel the turned lock is the technique to learn first so it is described first.

Turned Lock Weaving Technique

I will give the directions as if you were weaving my rug design. If you have designed your own, and I hope you have, adjust the count to suit your design. My count is: From the right side count off ten threads and mark the tenth with pencil, continue counting and mark the twenty-fifth, fortieth, fifty-fifth and seventieth warp ends. Starting on the left side do the same thing. This will leave thirteen warp ends in the middle section.

These marked warp ends are now considered the *turn* warp ends. In other words, the weft will turn around these warps each time the weft changes direction in the weaving. The turn threads may come either on the back or front of the batten.

We will assume you ended your horizontal stripe left to right and your weft is hanging on the right side. Therefore, you will add your new weft colors on the right of each pattern block. My colors are dark grey, light tan and white.

Fastening in New Weft Colors—We will give you three methods for fastening in new colors.

Method Number One—The rules are:

1. If turn warp is on *front* of batten, you hook weft yarn around it with *long* end toward direction of weaving.

2. If turn warp is on *back* of batten, you hook yarn around it with *short* end toward direction of weaving. (See photo N43.)

In our photographs we show the short ends

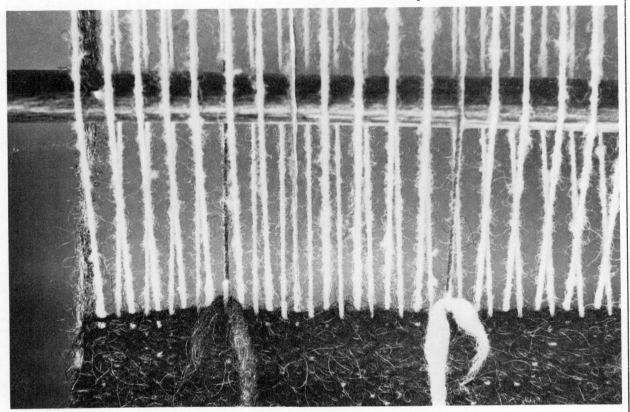

Photo N43. Fastening in new colors of weft, Method Number One. Short ends of weft are shown longer than necessary for clarity. Short ends should consist of just a few fibers. Note the tenth and twenty-fifth warp ends have been marked and designated as the turn warp ends.

much longer than they should be so you will have no difficulty in seeing what we are describing. In actual practice these short ends of weft should be just a few fibers of the tapered end of your weft yarn. As you weave you can snip off the fibers that hang out but they should be so few that the snipped area is impossible to detect.

Method Number Two—Turn batten vertically and with index finger pick up opposite shed for ½ " to left of turn warp end. With just a few fibers of the tapered end of your weft, weave left to right in this picked-up shed. These few fibers will be in the same shed as preceding weft. (See photo N44.)

Method Number Three—Some weavers just put weft into shed without fastening the end in any way.

I will use Method Number One for fastening in the new weft colors as this method clearly defines the turn warp thread being used. Now with the rules in mind,

Step 1—Insert batten in stick shed. Do not

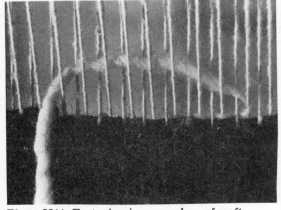

Photo N44. Fastening in new colors of weft, Method Number Two.

split selvage threads. Turn batten horizontally.

Step 2—We will be weaving to the left so on the tenth warp from the left, which is on *back* of batten, add dark grey weft with short end to left, the direction of the weaving. We will henceforth call this weft A.

Step 3—On the twenty-fifth warp from the left which is on the *front* of batten, add white weft with long end to the left. This will be weft B. (See photo N43.)

Step 4—Proceed across, hooking in weft C (dark grey), weft D (tan), weft E (dark grey), weft F (white), weft G (dark grey), weft H (tan), weft I (dark grey), weft J (white). The weft hanging to the right side of the weaving will be weft K (dark grey).

Now that you have all the wefts attached to your weaving there are several rules to memorize.

• When the weft yarns are hanging to the *right* of the design blocks, you begin weaving with the weft on the *left* and work to the right.

• When the weft ends are hanging to the *left* of the design blocks, you begin on the *right* and work *left*.

To make it easy, just remember opposites: Wefts on right, begin left. Wefts on left, begin right.

To weave vertical lines you must understand the following:

• If the turn warp end is on the *front* of the batten, the weft goes around *behind* it and into the shed, or comes out from *behind* it, depending on whether you are at the beginning or end of a design block.

• If the turn warp end is on the *back* of the batten, the weft always goes into the shed just in *front* of the turn warp end and comes out of the shed just in *front* of it.

When you understand these four rules, the turned lock method will be easy. To apply the rules refer to photo N45 and follow carefully with me word by word these instructions:

Step 1—Wefts are hanging to the *right* of the design blocks so we will begin weaving on the *left* with weft A.

Step 2—Weave weft A to the left as follows: Because the turn warp is on the *back* of the batten, we take weft A into the shed in front of the turn warp. Pull weft A snugly around the turn warp but keep it loose in the shed. Beat.

Step 3—Weave weft B to the left as follows: Because the turn warp is on the *front* of the batten, you take weft B to the right of the turn warp be-

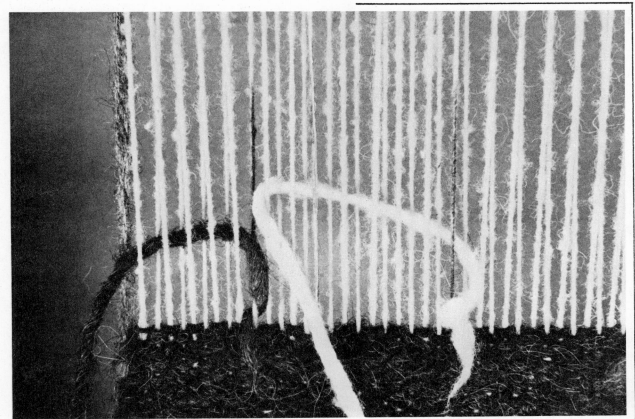

Photo N45. Weaving first row of pattern—the tenth and twenty-fifth warp ends are marked as the turn warp ends for beginning of pattern. Weft A is dark grey, weft B is white.

hind it and into the shed. Because at the end of the block the turn warp is on the *back* of the batten, you come out of the shed just in front of the turn warp.

Step 4—Weave weft C to the left applying the proper rules. Continue across until all wefts are woven and ends are hanging on left. Remove batten.

Step 5—Change to pull shed, insert batten. Split selvage threads, turn batten horizontally.

Step 6—Weft ends on left so begin weaving on right with weft K. Weave left to right with wefts K, J, I, H, G, F, E, D, C, B and A. Follow with me for the weaving of wefts C, B and A. For weft C the turn warp is on the *back* of the batten so it goes into the shed just in front of this turn warp and it comes out of the shed from behind the turn warp at end of pattern block over weft D. Weft B goes into the shed to the left and behind the turn warp which is on *front* of batten and comes out of shed in front of turn warp on back of batten at end of pattern block. Weft A goes into shed from edge and comes out from behind turn warp on *front* of batten over weft B at end of block. (See photo N46.)

Confused? Don't be. Now is a good time to reread the four rules. If you are doing this correctly,

Photo N46. Weaving second row of pattern —Wefts A, B, C, D shown. Wefts are unbeaten for clarity.

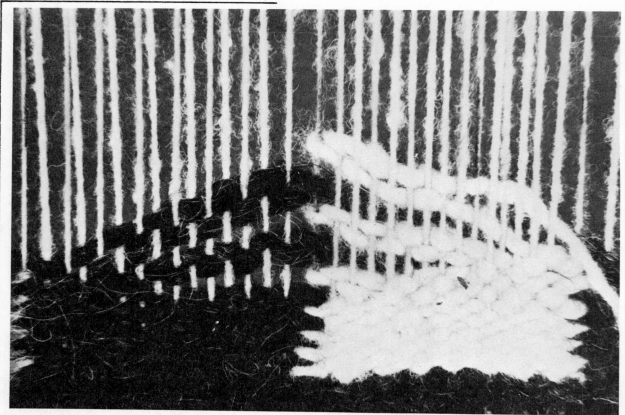

Photo N47. Detail of turned lock method—
Wefts reverse on same warp end.

wefts of adjacent blocks are turning on same warp thread. (See photo N47.)

To repeat some words of caution, pull weft snugly around turn warp but not so tightly that turn warp is pulled out of position. Get a lot of weft into shed even though the areas are small. Warp will loosen some as you weave so adjust tension when necessary. Don't let low places develop. Fill in at once and keep level of weaving even.

Advancing Pattern to Right and Left—We have now woven ¾″ of our first pattern blocks. *Note:* It is advisable to weave two more rows after you have your measurement as the last rows will pack down with subsequent weaving. We now wish to advance weft C to the left over weft B and narrow the white area. We want to end weft F pattern block as it is now completed.

We must mark new turn warp ends. From left count over and mark the sixteenth warp end. Repeat on right side. Refer to photo N48 and work as follows:

Step 1——Make shed. Insert batten. From here on we will omit directions on selvage threads but you continue to weave them as described previously.

Step 2——Weft ends are on the right so we begin on the left and weave weft A right to left.

Step 3——Weave weft B right to left.

Step 4——Weft C must now advance to the left

over weft B to the new turn warp. There will be two wefts in the shed at the point of advancement. (See photo N48.)

Step 5—Weave weft D.

Step 6—Weave weft E.

Step 7—Untwist and break off weft F so you have just a half inch of tapered yarn. Twist these fibers a little and lay in shed.

Step 8—Break off weft G to a length that will carry over weft F and into the area of weft E. Weave.

Step 9—Weave wefts H, I, J, K.

Step 10—Change shed. Insert batten. Turn batten horizontally.

Step 11—Weft ends are all on the left so we begin on the right with weft K. Weave weft K to right edge.

Step 12—Weave weft J to right.

Step 13—Weft I now advances over weft J to new turn warp.

Step 14—Weave weft H.

Step 15—Weave weft E over to meet weft H block.

Step 16—Weave weft D.

Step 17—Weave weft C, which is a wider block now.

Step 18—Weave weft B which is a narrower block now.

Photo N48. Advancing pattern to left: weft C over weft B. How to end a color: weft F ended, weft G over weft F and ending in weft E area. Weft E will now weave areas of E, F, G.

Step 19—Weave weft A.

The rule to remember: You can only advance in the direction you are weaving. You can advance left when you are weaving left and vice versa. At the point of advancement there are two wefts in the shed.

Continue weaving using these new turn warps until your wefts B, D, H and J measure 1⅞". You will then finish off wefts B and J and advance wefts D and H to right and left to enlarge these blocks. For these advancements you will mark the twenty-fifth and seventieth warps from each edge. Referring to the design layout on page 27, continue until you reach the beginning of the diagonal lines.

When you get to the center stripe of three warp ends only, to keep this area smooth pull fairly tightly on weft E to prevent the fabric from bulging out at this point.

Your selvage threads should be shaping up as shown in photo N41. If not, you may not be twisting them properly. If warp threads are closer together in some areas than others or if you are getting spaces around your turn warps and/or getting a heavy ridge at the vertical line or if your rug is narrowing in and if you are getting loops on surface refer to When Problems Develop section, page 77.

Weaving Diagonal Lines—You are now to part C of your design and diagonal lines. We will give you information on weaving the flat diamond in the center and you can apply this information to all your diagonal lines in this design.

Weaving diagonal lines may seem complicated but it will not be if you have learned your preceding lessons. Do not try diagonal lines until you understand thoroughly the rules relating to the turn warp ends. If you can weave vertical lines without getting confused, then you are ready for the diagonal. The rules are exactly the same; the only difference is that the turn warp ends change every other row of weaving instead of every few inches.

To begin the diamond (weft on right, stick shed):

Step 1—Find center warp thread.

Step 2—If center warp is on *front* of batten, hook the weft around this warp end with the long end toward the direction of the weaving. Because we are now dividing our center area with the diamond, we have to add another dark grey weft on one side of it.

To weave this first row of the diamond, just take the long end of the weft around the center warp end and out to the front again. Weave other wefts as usual. Change shed. Center warp is now on back of batten.

Step 3—Each warp end to the right and left of the diamond now becomes a turn warp end in succession. That is, the grey weft will turn on the warp end *next* to the center one, then the white will turn on this same warp over the grey. Then the grey will turn on the *second* warp end from the center and the white will turn on that same warp over the grey, etc. Each warp end becomes a turn warp. (See photo N49.) What you are actually

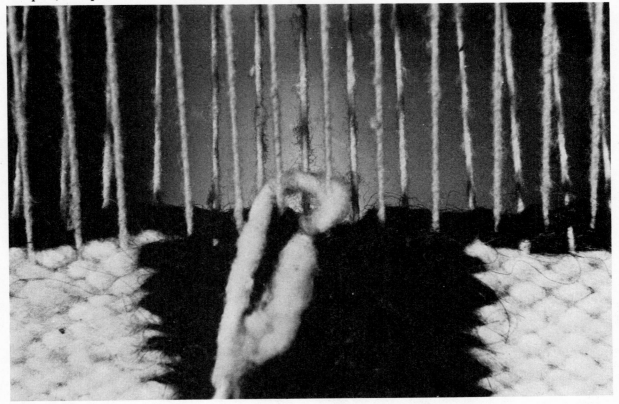

Photo N49. Beginning the diamond. White weft turns over black weft.

achieving are adjoining wefts turning back on adjoining warps. (See photo N11.)

If center warp is on *back* of batten, fasten weft on warp with long end hanging to right. Add another grey weft on left side. Weave all wefts left of center to left as usual. The grey weft just added will turn on the first warp to left of center warp. Weave the diamond weft one warp to left coming out over grey weft. Weave wefts on right of center to left as usual. (See photo N11 for diamond detail.)

The way to remember this, when weaving the diagonal line, is to ask yourself: Which warp end did the grey turn on last time? Actually put your finger on it. Then say to yourself, the next warp end to this is now the turn warp end, and then move your finger over to this one. Now apply the rule, if this new turn warp is on the *back* of the batten, the weft goes into the shed just in front of it or if this new turn warp end is on the *front* of the batten, the weft goes around behind it and into the shed. These are the same rules you have been using. After weaving, look to see if the weft did turn on the correct warp end.

Until you are sure of what you are doing, always check each time before you continue. Because you are weaving a diamond with a diagonal on each side, you have to ask yourself these questions and determine the turn warp end for each side of the diamond. Be slow and methodical when you begin and soon you won't have to think so much about it. You will know just what to do.

Step 4—To change the direction of the diagonal, turn *three* wefts on the same turn warp; that is, we have reached the widest point of our diamond and we now have a grey, then a white weft turning on the same warp end. To change direction of the diagonal line the next grey weft should turn on this same warp end over the white diamond weft. This now gives us a grey, white, grey turning on same warp. From here on to the finish of the diamond the white diamond weft turns first on each warp end and the grey turns over the white. The turn warp ends are now advancing toward the center. (See photo N50.)

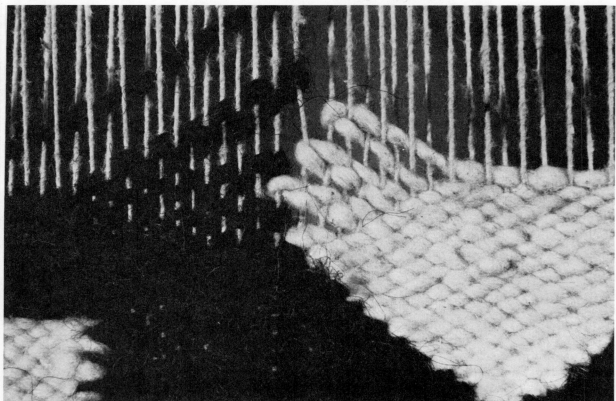

Photo N50. Changing the direction of the diagonal line—three wefts turn on same warp and the grey weft now turns *over* the white.

With the completion of the center diamond, you have passed the center of your rug and are now reversing your pattern. You may have discovered that the center of your diamond didn't come quite to the halfway point of your warp or maybe you got to the halfway point of the warp before you reached the center of your diamond. If it came out exactly right, you are to be congratulated.

The chances are, before you reached the halfway mark you were looking ahead and could determine that some slight change would have to be made to get the design to balance. Most Navajo weavers feel that it is best to adjust the design somewhere in the middle rather than have the ends of the rug unbalanced.

Interlock Weaving Technique

The interlock method of weaving can be very simple if you have an even number of warp threads. If you have an odd number of warp threads, it becomes more complicated. I would suggest that if you have not at this point set up your warp and you want to do the interlocking method, you wind an even number. If your warp is already wound with an odd number of warp ends, then put one extra warp in one edge group so you are for all intents and purposes working with even pairs. Most Navajo weavers prefer to work with even pairs.

Since our sample rug was first planned for the turned lock method with odd number of warp ends, we added one extra warp thread to right edge warp count so we could work with pairs. Our directions are given accordingly, based on 152 warp ends. A few photographs we have used were taken of a loom with a similar setup but not exactly the same warp count as the sample rug. Don't worry if the warp count doesn't agree in all photos. It's the technique we are showing. Also, since we have discussed the weaving of the Navajo selvage with the turned lock method, we will not repeat. Review this before starting your weaving (page 48).

The interlock method has its own set of rules so don't confuse them with the rules for the turned lock method.

The first thing you must do after weaving your initial stripe area is to mark your warp. Either tie in colored yarns or mark with pencil. For clarity we have marked our warp with pencil. You will need to mark two warp ends for each vertical line of color. The weft will interlock *between* these two.

Mark warps 9 and 10, 23 and 24, 39 and 40, 53 and 54, 69 and 70 from each edge ignoring one warp on right edge if you have an odd number of warp threads.

With the interlock method you always begin your weaving from the same edge. However you set it up is the way it should continue. Our directions are for beginning on the right side.

Refer to design on diagram N2. After you

finish your stripe area, end with weft on left. It takes two rows to complete an interlock. I will refer to one row as the interlock row and the other as the completion of the interlock or completion row.

Row 1—Weft A on left. Pull shed on my loom. First warp on right, not counting the one extra we mentioned above, is on back of batten. Weave this extra one but don't count it. Begin on right edge and lay in and weave to the right the new colors, wefts K, J, I, H, G, F, E, D, C, B each area beginning and ending between the pairs of marked warp ends. Weave weft A at left edge also. Now all wefts are hanging on right of design blocks.

Row 2—Stick shed. Beginning on right side, weave to left bringing weft K to the front between warps 9 and 10. Drop weft K over weft J. Pick up weft J from under weft K and take weft J between warps 9 and 10 through the shed and out between warps 23 and 24. Drop weft J over weft I. Pick up weft I from under weft J and continue across interlocking the wefts. Ends are on left side. You have just completed the interlock row.

Row 3—Pull shed. Beginning on right again, weave first weft K, then weft J, then I, etc. Wefts do not interlock on this row. This is the completion of the interlock row.

Row 4—Stick shed. Proceed as you did for Row 2. This is an interlock row.

Row 5—Pull shed. Proceed as you did for Row 3. This is a completion row. Wefts always enter and emerge from the shed between the marked warp pairs. (See photos N51, N52, N53.) You are beginning every row with weft K on the right.

As the interlock method has a tendency to have a ridge at the point of interlock be sure to pull the weft snug at this point so the locking wefts will lay smoothly *between* the warp threads. Continue until you have ¾″ woven. Areas B, C, I and J now change shape.

Advancing Pattern to Right and Left—You must begin your design change in the completion row each time. To enlarge one area means you decrease another. On the completion row you can advance a color area in the direction you are weaving and you can decrease in preparation for advancing on the interlock row. On the interlock row you can advance the direction you are weaving only over a decrease area left from the completion row. You cannot decrease on the interlock row. It takes two rows to complete a design change.

End with an interlock row. Mark warps 15 and 16 from each edge and then follow with me: Wefts are on left. Pull shed. A completion row with design change:

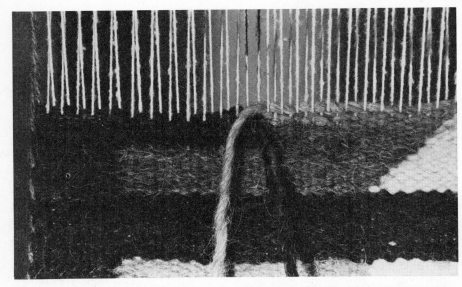

Photo N51. Interlock Method, Step 1, Interlock row—Beginning with weft on right and weaving right to left interlocking tan weft with grey weft. Note marked warp threads.

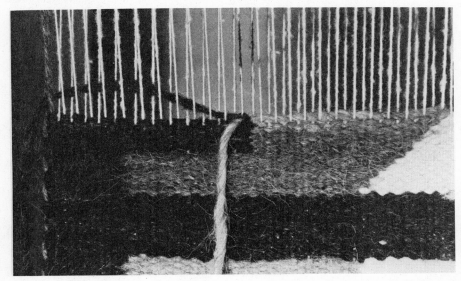

Photo N52. Interlock Method, Step 2—Picking up grey weft from underneath tan weft and weaving to left.

Photo N53. Interlock Method, Step 3—Completion of interlock which we call the completion row. Beginning on right and weaving left to right. The tan weft completes the lock between marked warp threads.

Row 1—Weave wefts K and J as usual. Weave weft I to right over weft J to new interlock point between warps 15 and 16. (Same idea as shown in photo N48 for turned lock method.) Weave weft H. Fasten off wefts G and F and weave weft E over wefts F and G. Weave wefts D and C. Weave weft B to new interlocking point between warps 15 and 16. We are leaving a small area unwoven decreasing weft B area in preparation for advancing weft C on next row. Weave weft A.

Row 2—Wefts on right. Stick shed. Interlock row and second row of design change: Begin on right and weave to left wefts K, J, I, H, E and D. Weave weft C over weft B and emerge between warps 15 and 16 and interlock with weft B at this point. Weave weft B, then A. The design change has now been established. (See photos N54 and N55.)

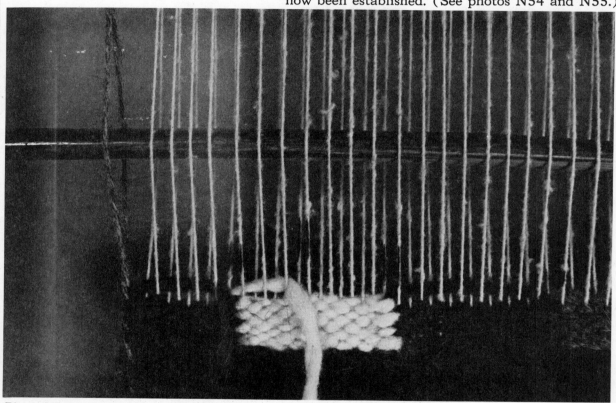

Photo N54. Interlock Method—Decreasing weft B area in preparation for advancing weft C area.

When you write on a subject you wonder sometimes how much detail you really should include. For some, too much detail is confusing and for others not enough has the same result. For those of you who are interested in the finer points I would like to add the following comment. I have chosen to give the interlocking instructions to achieve the same result as shown in a drawing in Gladys Reichard's book *Navajo Shepherd and Weaver*. When you look at the interlocking point of the two wefts as given above, you will find that on the first row of the two rows making the interlock the two wefts turn back *over* the two adjoining warps

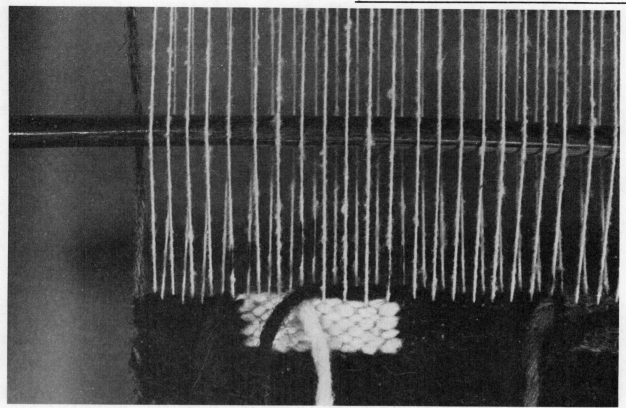

Photo N55. Interlock Method—Advancing weft C over weft B. There is a double weft in shed at point of advancement.

and on the second row they go *under* the two adjoining warps. (See photo N12, a close-up of interlock joint.) This is because our count put the first warp of the marked pairs on an odd-numbered warp from the edge, such as 9 and 10. If you were to put the first marked warp of the pairs on an even number from the edge, for instance 10 and 11, there would be an exact opposite result (the same as viewing photo N12 upside down). That is, on the first row the two wefts would turn back *under* the adjoining warps and on the second row go *over* the adjoining warps. Either way you get the same end result. I have been unable to determine which way is preferred among the Navajo weavers.

To summarize:
• Wefts interlock *between* warps.
• Wefts interlock on one row, not on the next.
• You begin weaving from the same side each time.
• Design change must begin on completion row.
• Pull wefts snugly at interlock but keep loose in shed.

Combining Weaving Methods

The rules we have just covered will remain the same until you reach the diagonal line in the design. How to weave a diagonal line is explained in the section on the turned lock method. When you combine techniques, you have two sets of rules to remember.

You have just finished the area with five wefts and you are ready to add the white just in from each edge and the white for the diagonal on either side of the center vertical stripe. Since the diagonal will be woven using the turned lock method, our project will be divided into three areas. If you are using my colors, you will have from left to right grey, white, grey weaving the interlock method on both sides of the blocks. Then the tan will be woven with the interlock method on left side and turned lock method on right side. White will be woven with the turned lock method on left side and interlock on right side. Center grey will be interlock on both sides and the white, tan, grey, white, grey will be the reverse on other side of rug. Therefore, you must take each area separately.

With the weft ends on the left, add your four new white wefts and weave to right. We now have from left to right wefts A, B, C, D, E, F, G, H, I, J and K. All ends are on right. We are ready to weave the interlocking row. We will weave the area on the left first.

Step 1—From the left move to the right to the first line that is not to be interlocking. That will be the white diagonal.

Step 2—Starting at the right *from this point* weave weft D, C, B and A, interlocking as usual.

Step 3—Now take center area and move to right until you reach the next non-interlocking line. This will be the other white diagonal.

Step 4—Beginning on right at this point white weft G interlocks with black weft F. Weft F interlocks with white weft E. Weave weft E which does not interlock with any.

Step 5—Take the area on the right, and beginning on right weave and interlock wefts K, J, I and H. You cannot interlock H with G because G is already woven.

Step 6—Ends are on left. Weave completion row. Begin on right and weave wefts K, J, I, etc. on across the row.

Continue weaving your design reversing at the center. Plan ahead so if adjustments in your design are necessary, you can decide before reaching the midpoint.

Finishing the Rug

No matter what method you have chosen to weave your rug, the following rules apply for finishing.

1. Somewhere shortly beyond the halfway mark you should weave the last four rows of weaving. This is done in the same manner as the first

four rows except you beat the weft up instead of down. Do not include selvage threads. (See photo N56.)

2. As the weaving progresses, the warp gets tighter and tighter so we change our tools. First change to a narrower batten and use that for a while. Keep going to smaller battens. After a while don't try to turn the batten horizontally. Just let the thickness of it make your shed.

3. A very tight twist is building up with your selvage threads. Untie at top, release some of the twist and retie with correct tension.

4. As the warp gets tighter, change to a smaller shed stick. I changed from a $\frac{3}{8}''$ to a $\frac{3}{16}''$ dowel. (See photo N57.)

5. Soon you will not be able to beat as usual. You may want to use a smaller comb. Since you can't beat, you have to press the weft into place. Do this by using a rocking motion across the weaving. From the bound end of weft press with edge of comb, then let it come down flat on the weaving. (See photos N58 and N59.)

6. You will soon want to change to an even smaller shed stick. Use a wire like a coat hanger wire. It makes a small shed but it's there and you can find it. (See photo N60.)

7. You can no longer get your fingers into the shed to move the weft. The Navajo often uses a small reed. She breaks the end so it is rough, then

Photo N56. Last three rows picked up and woven, fourth row picked up and weft being drawn through shed. Do not include selvage threads.

Photo N57. As warp tightens, change to smaller batten and smaller shed stick. We are using ³⁄₁₆″ dowel now.

Photo N58. When there is no room to beat, use a rocking, pressing motion with comb. Press with edge of comb then . . .

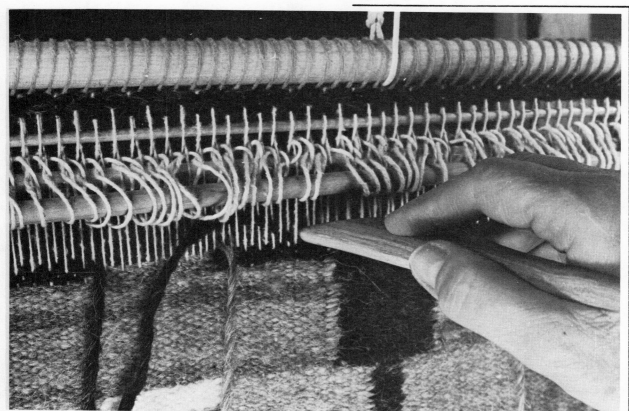

Photo N59. . . . lower comb flat on weaving. Work across, pulling extra weft into shed as comb comes down to weaving.

Photo N60. The warp continues to tighten. Change to a wire for a shed stick.

Photo N61. Using a small reed for a shuttle in a tight shed

Photo N62. Using bag or sack needles to carry weft through tight shed

wets it with her tongue, touches the weft to this rough wet end and twists it in her fingers thus winding a few inches of yarn onto it. This she puts into the small shed. (See photo N61.)

She may also use bag or sack needles to carry the weft through the shed. (See photo N62.)

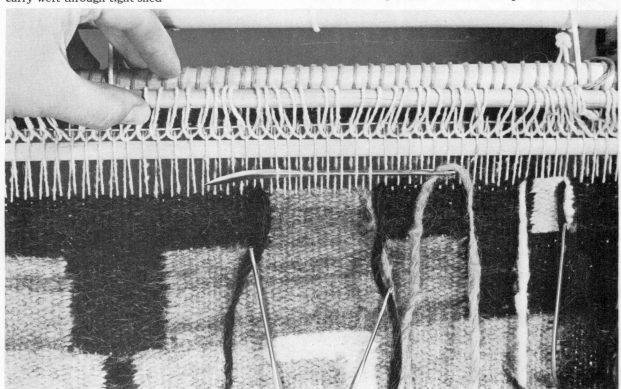

At this point we should caution you about pulling your handspun weft through a tight shed. Since you are working with short lengths of yarn, I'm sure you have noticed that it comes unspun. It is wise to twist it a few times before you weave it. If you don't keep the same amount of twist in the yarn, the end of the rug will not look like the beginning. Also it will be more difficult to see to pick up the sheds when the heddle stick is removed.

8. It is now impossible to use the heddle stick. Slip stick out of the heddles and remove the heddle string. Be careful in pulling out the heddle string

Photo N63. Removing heddles

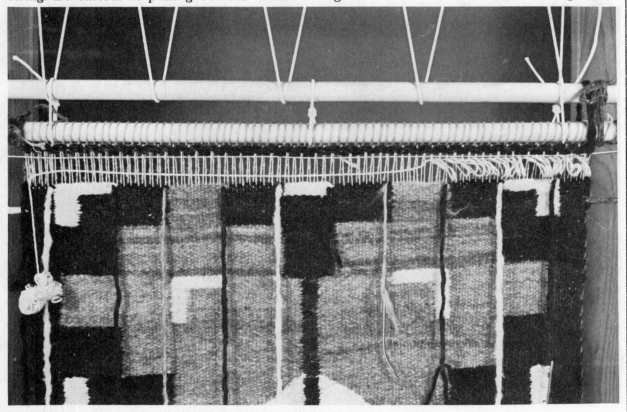

or you will weaken or break a warp thread. Pull it out to the side so you do not put pressure on the edge warps. (See photo N63.)

9. You now have to pick up your sheds with the wire shed stick thread by thread. However, for each pick-up made you can weave two rows of weft, one above the stick and one below. You are now weaving down from the top and up from the bottom. Don't forget your selvage threads as you weave up. Do not include them as you weave down. (See photo N64.)

10. Your warp is now so tight and the weaving space so small that it is difficult to use the teeth of your comb to press the weft into place. Use the point of the comb to push weft into place. Even though the shed is tight be sure to get plenty of weft into it. The end of your rug will narrow down

Photo N64. Shed is picked up with wire, then one row is woven above and one row below.

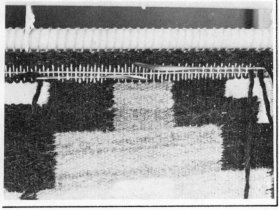

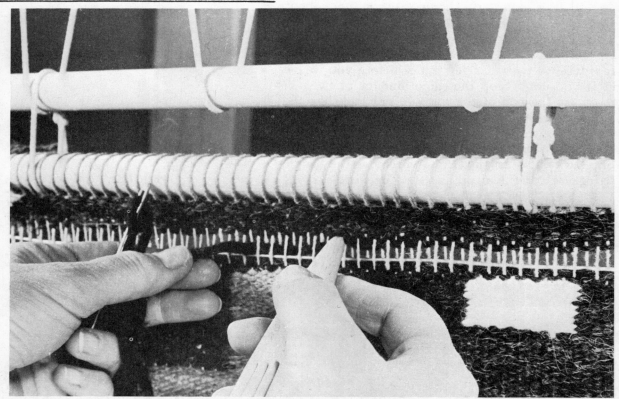

Photo N65. Use point of comb to push weft into place.

considerably if you don't. This is slow, tedious weaving but must be done carefully. (See photo N65.)

11. When you get to the last ½″ of your weaving, you will have to abandon the shed stick. Do your shed pick-up with the sack needle. Pick up just a few warp threads at a time, three or four, and pull weft through. However, the tension is very tight and you must pull the weft through from side to side, keeping your fingers on the fabric so there is as little friction as possible. If you pull the weft holding hands away from the weaving, you will most likely break a warp thread or two and damage your weft yarn.

Pulling the weft through builds up the twist of the yarn on the bound side of the weft yarn. As you come to the end of the slack, slow down your pulling motion and do not draw the weft tightly. With the point of your comb try to distribute the twist that has built up and push the weft down (or up, as the case may be) in between almost every warp thread. This will help to get enough weft in the shed so it does not pull in and let warp show.

Use short lengths of weft so you do not have to pull the same weft through the shed too many times. If the lengths are too long, you will notice that your weft gradually becomes soft and weak. This is because most of the twist is being forced into the area close to the bound end. Don't try to

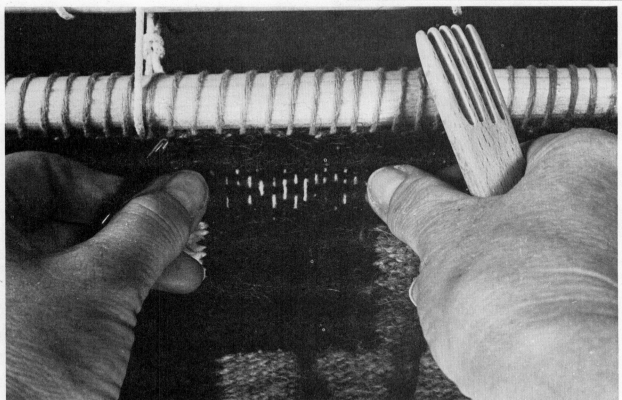

Photo N66. Carefully pull weft through shed keeping fingers on fabric to eliminate undue wear on warp and weft.

hurry this last bit of weaving. It takes time any way you do it so a little more time to make it right should be allowed. (See photo N66.)

12. To get short ends of weft into the shed, make a yarn loop on a needle, hook weft into loop and pull needle, loop and weft through shed. (See photo N67.)

13. When you get to the last few rows, you have to really work at getting the weft into the shed. Use the point of your comb to find the right warp threads and pick them up with your sack needle. Weave only a few threads at a time. As mentioned before, when you have pulled your weft through the shed, use the point of your comb to push it into place between each warp thread. When you push with the point of comb, do so toward the bound end of the weft so that with each little push you draw some weft into the shed. After a while you will be picking up one thread at a time but this is the way it has to be. Each time you pick up your sack needle remember to twist it a time or two to respin the yarn. (See photo N68.)

14. When you think you can't get any more weft into the shed, put in four more rows. A good rug must have as much weft in the end as at the beginning.

15. You come to a point where you have two wefts in the same shed and you can't get any more in. You will make one more row of pick-up and

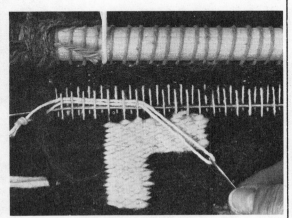

Photo N67. To get short ends of weft into the shed, make a yarn loop on a needle, hook weft in loop and pull into shed.

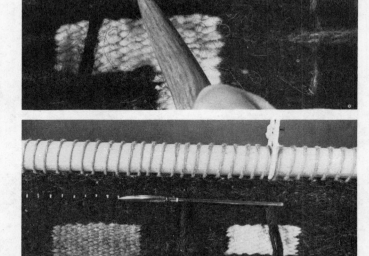

Photo N68. Using sack needle and point of comb to help pick up correct warp threads, weave only a few warps at a time.

Photo N69. Weaving the last row—on the left you see two wefts in the same shed, on the right the last row separates these two wefts and finishes the rug.

this will separate the two wefts in the same shed and finish your rug. (See photo N69.)

Removing Rug from Loom

Step 1—Untie tension cord and remove.

Step 2—Remove three cord ties at top and three at bottom.

Step 3—Untie selvage cords and end of warp yarn if this is tied to dowels.

Step 4—Remove binding cord that laces rug to dowels being careful not to break the twining cord. The Navajo uses the point of her comb to help pull this cord out. She carefully winds the cord into a little ball for use on her next rug. DO NOT REMOVE THE TWINING CORD.

Since the selvage threads could not be woven in at the very top while you were weaving down, you will weave them in with a sack needle in the same manner as you wove them throughout the rug. (See photo N70.)

Take the two ends of the twining cord and the two ends of the selvage cord and knot them together at the corners. If you didn't weave in the warp loop on first thread, thread in a needle and work it into rug or tie this warp end in with the corner tie.

Analyzing Your Navajo Rug

As mentioned earlier, this rug was intended as an example to incorporate all the problems that confront a beginning weaver on her first attempt at Navajo-type weaving. I worked in quite a few problems and one or two I didn't plan on.

Throw your rug on the floor and have a good look at it. It may look just beautiful to you and this is as it should be, just as long as you are not fooling yourself that you did a perfect job of weaving the first time. Walk around it, view it from different angles with a critical eye. Now let's analyze our rugs together. (See photo N71.)

• Is the width across each end the same? Fold one end over the other and check. My rug is narrower at the top by about ⅝". I have seen rugs that varied over 2" and it was quite evident. The eye may not discern a small variation in width on a large-size rug. As you weave keep checking the width and begin corrective measures as soon as you see a change.

• Do you see any wrinkles in your rug? Mine is fairly smooth even when out of the loom. If you have wrinkled areas, you were probably not pulling your weft tightly enough at the interlock or turned lock point. If you were weaving tightly for a while and then for some reason started weaving with much more weft in the shed, ripples may have

Photo N71. The finished product incorporating problems confronting a new weaver on her first attempt at Navajo type weaving.

developed. Wrinkles and ripples usually are the result of incorrect tensions.

• The edges should be straight. Are yours? Mine aren't too bad. Here again uneven edges are a result of incorrect weft and warp tension.

• Does your rug lie flat on the floor? Possibly your selvage threads were woven too tightly or your weaving was wider than the twining at the beginning and end and the corners tend to cup. If you stretched the twining greatly in mounting it on the loom dowel, it will contract when tension is off and be narrower than the weaving. If the selvage threads are too tight, you can easily ease them but it's a little more difficult to ease the twining cords.

• Are there any floats in your rug where the weft skipped over more than one warp end? I must admit I have one skip in my rug. You should be careful when you insert the batten into the shed. Don't pick up any warps from the back as you place the batten.

• Are the horizontal and vertical lines straight as well as uniform in width? You must turn between or around the correct warps each time to keep your lines straight.

• Is the warp visible? It shouldn't be. The weft should cover it completely. If it shows in some areas, you were probably pulling your weft too tight and not getting enough in the shed. Because of my uneven yarn I had difficulty covering my warp in some areas.

• Is your rug streaked because of uneven color in yarn? Mine is very much. The tan yarn was not evenly carded and the mixing of the two colors was very uneven. There were many thick and thin areas because of poor spinning and I spent a lot of time filling in the low places—good practice but time consuming. Such variations in the yarn distort the design blocks.

• In my rug, the outer white diamond has a bow in the upper right of the diagonal line. The white yarn I was using for this area was thicker and more tightly spun than the white used for the left side. I switched to a thinner yarn and completed the diagonal. This is one of the best examples of what unevenly spun yarn will do to your design. Each color of weft should be the same thickness and twist.

• We cautioned against having blunt ends of weft showing. In the first half of the rug I had left extra long short ends for clarity in my photographs and I just snipped them off even with the rug surface. You can see how it shows at the lower corners of the white blocks. These short ends should be just a few fibers and thereby not show at all.

• Look at the overall design. My original

plan was to have the center horizontal black area the same width as the center vertical area. However, after I got started, I decided that the vertical stripe was too narrow and so I adjusted the size of the diamond to give a wider stripe at this point. I think it would have come out slightly wider anyway. Be sure to look ahead a little and if your design isn't working out as planned, decide on the adjustment before you get to the exact spot or it will be too late to work out something that will succeed.

My first and last stripe are just about the same. If you haven't been careful in measuring, the last stripe will be a different width from the first one. A little variation is not objectionable but it shouldn't be too obvious.

• The first half of this rug was woven using the turned lock method and the last half was woven with the interlock method. You can readily see the difference.

Now who will be the first to walk upon your rug?

When Problems Develop

We suggest where possible that when problems develop you take the weaving out and do it over. However, most of the time this entails much work so we offer other solutions.

• *If warp does not hang in separate loops from the twining cord after mounting in loom frame,* you have erred in binding your warp to the loom rod. Solution: Undo binding cord and correct. A common error is to bind one loop ahead of the next loop thereby getting warp threads twisted. Be sure to bind warp loops in proper order. Check the cross to find right order if you are unsure.

• *If the twining cord pulls away from the loom dowel rod and has a scalloped look at the ends after mounting in loom frame,* you have not wrapped the binding cord tightly enough. This should have been corrected before weaving was started. Solution: Undo binding cord and tighten.

• *If the tension on your warp is uneven after you stretch it in the loom,* you probably were not careful enough in winding the warp. Solution: Beginning at the edge of the loose area, work across this area pulling each warp thread to the right tension, easing it through the twining cord and working the looseness to the nearest edge. If necessary, untie outside warp thread and remove excess length of warp.

• *If you have two warp threads weaving like a double thread,* you have erred in making your heddles. There should be a heddle around every other warp thread. Solution: Insert batten in pull

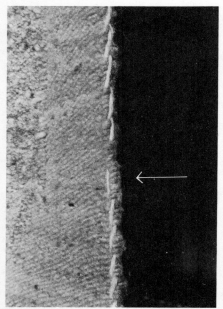

Photo N72. Selvage threads incorrectly twisted at one point.

shed, making sure alternate warp threads are on front of batten; that is, warp threads on back of shed stick should be on front of batten. Undo heddles to error and correct. Also check to be sure that the error is not caused by the shed stick being inserted improperly.

• *If in the beginning your stick shed is too small,* your heddles are too short. Solution: Take out and redo your heddles.

• *If you can see warp peeking through the weft,* you are pulling your weft too tight. Solution: Ease up on weft tension. Get a lot in the shed.

• *If your weaving line is uneven,* (a) your weft yarn is not evenly spun or (b) you are drawing in and weft will not beat down where warps are too close together. Solution: Fill in low places as they develop. (See Things to Know Before You Start to Weave, page 42.) If possible, change to more evenly spun yarn. Get more weft in shed and be sure warp is tight.

• *If you have weft floats on the surface,* you have not been accurate in making your shed. You may have a heddle longer than others that is holding a warp thread out of line or you may have picked up incorrect threads in working weft through the shed with your fingers. Solution: To correct this: (a) When you insert your batten be sure the point does not pick up warp threads from the back. (b) All heddles must be the same length. Adjust. (c) Be careful in passing the weft through the shed.

• *If your selvage threads are not uniformly twisted* (as in photo N72), you are not twisting them properly. Solution: Refer to Things to Know Before You Start to Weave—Navajo Selvage (page 48).

• *If you have loops of weft on the surface,* you are getting too much weft in the shed. Solution: Put a little more tension on weft as you beat it down. If you are bubbling with the point of your comb, you are pressing too hard with the point.

• *If your batten keeps snapping back to vertical position,* your warp is too loose. Solution: A very tight warp is necessary at all times. Adjust tension.

• *If your vertical lines are not straight,* you have turned on or between the wrong warp thread or threads. Solution: Review the rules for the weaving method you are using.

• *If your diagonal lines are not straight,* you have turned on the wrong warp threads and/or you changed to a different size or twist of weft yarn. Solution: Review rules for weaving diagonal lines, and make sure you use the same size and twist of yarn throughout.

• *If your rug is drawing in and width is narrower than when you began,* (a) you are not getting enough weft in the shed or (b) warp is too loose. Solution: About ½″ below weaving line on each side, add a heavy cord about ½″ in from edge. Tie to loom frame, stretching rug to correct width. If necessary, add more ties every few inches. (See photo N73.)

• *If the warp separates at the vertical lines and/or ridges develop,* (a) you are pulling too much on the weft yarns and drawing warp out of position, (b) you are not pulling enough on the weft and it is too loose around the turn warp or loose where it interlocks between warps, (c) your warp is too loose allowing the weft to dominate the tension or (d) in passing the yarn through the shed your fingers are continually forcing an opening at this point. The solutions are: (a) When some warps become more open, it means others are closer together. You must redistribute the space. Grasp warp with both hands dividing warps first on one side of open area and then on the other side. By pulling some warps one way and others another, rearrange the position of the warps so they are evenly spaced. (See photos N74, N75 and N76.) (b) Try not to move the warps as you handle the weft.

Photo N73. If weaving is narrowing, add ties on edge and stretch out to correct width.

Photo N74. The problem: Space has developed at the vertical line.

Photo N75. The solution: Rearrange position of warp ends.

Photo N76. Problem solved: Warps are evenly spaced again.

• *If warp threads become closer together in some areas,* (a) you are not getting enough weft into the shed, (b) you are pulling weft too tight in pattern areas, (c) you are weaving with warp too loose or (d) weft is too thick and will not pack down between the warp threads.

One solution is: (a) With point of comb lift weft to open up the weaving. (b) With point of comb push warps from side to side forcing more space between. Don't be gentle but on the other hand you can break a thread if you overdo it. (See photo N77.) (c) Beat weft into place.

A second solution is: (a) Lift weft to open up the weaving. (b) Grasp the warp with both hands at different places and pull warps apart. (See photo N75 and solution (a) to the preceding problem.) (c) Beat weft into place.

A third solution is for very drastic cases only and should never be necessary after you've had time to learn the fundamentals.

Remove two warp threads. Cut one in the middle of the problem area. Pull it out of heddle and twining and cut it again close to weaving. (See photos N78 and N79.) Grasp the warp with both hands as in photo N75 and space out the remaining warps. Adjust warp spacing at top twining. One heddle is now empty so you have to adjust heddle string and distribute the extra length among the other heddles.

Photo N77. Lifting wefts and with point of comb moving warps from side to side to get more space around them.

Photo N78. When warps become close together in some areas, you can remove two warp threads. This is recommended only for very drastic cases. Cut one warp thread.

Photo N79. Pull warp thread out of twining and heddle and cut off, thereby removing two warp threads.

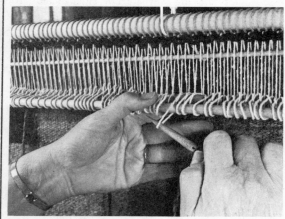

Photo N80. Adjusting length of heddles

• *If the length of some heddles becomes short,* (a) the heddle string loop is too tight around the heddle rod and as you handle the heddle rod it twists and heddle string wraps around end thus shortening string and heddles. (b) If some heddles become longer and some shorter, you are probably sticking your fingers through the heddles as you use the pull shed thus putting pressure on some. When you lengthen one, you shorten another. With point of comb and holding heddle rod as when you made the heddles, work from the left to adjust heddle to original length. (See photo N80.)

• *If a warp thread breaks,* you had a weak spot in your warp or too much pressure was put on it in weaving or making corrections. (a) Tie on a new length of warp with a secure knot, bring warp through twining and heddle area as it was before it broke, then either: tie warp end to bottom of loom frame at same tension as other warp and continue weaving (the end should be worked into rug after it is complete and off the loom) or thread a tapestry needle with warp end and weave the end into the rug. (See photos N81 and N82.) (b) Bury the knot in the weft when you come to it in the weaving.

• *If you remove your shed and heddle stick for some reason or they fall out by accident,* insert

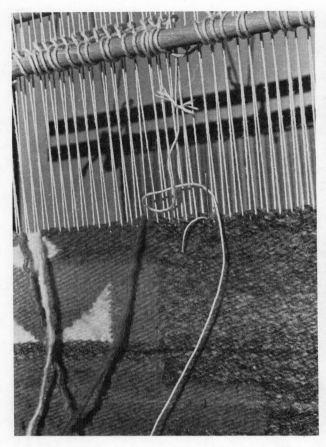

Photo N81. Tie on a length of warp to broken thread and thread in tapestry needle. Take the point of needle into weaving beside other end of broken warp, then . . .

Photo N82. . . . pull new warp length through fabric. Tighten to same tension as other warp threads.

the shed stick first so there is no twist between shed stick and top twining. The shed stick should be cradled in the loops of the warp. When shed stick has been inserted correctly, pick up warp ends on the back of shed stick with batten and make a heddle around these warps.

Photo N78 shows shed and heddle sticks inserted in opposite sheds from where they were at the beginning. You can see a twist between shed stick and top twining. You can weave with them this way but it can be confusing if you change in the middle of a project.

• *If you develop aches and pains as you weave,* sit higher or lower in relation to your weaving. You shouldn't have to reach too high to do the weaving.

The Lazy Line

I'm sure most of you have heard the term lazy line in reference to a Navajo rug but many of you may not understand the meaning.

The Navajo weaves a width that is comfortable for her without moving from side to side each time she does a row. If the rug is wider than a comfortable weaving width, she weaves the area in front of her, then moves over and catches the other areas up to where she stopped with the first

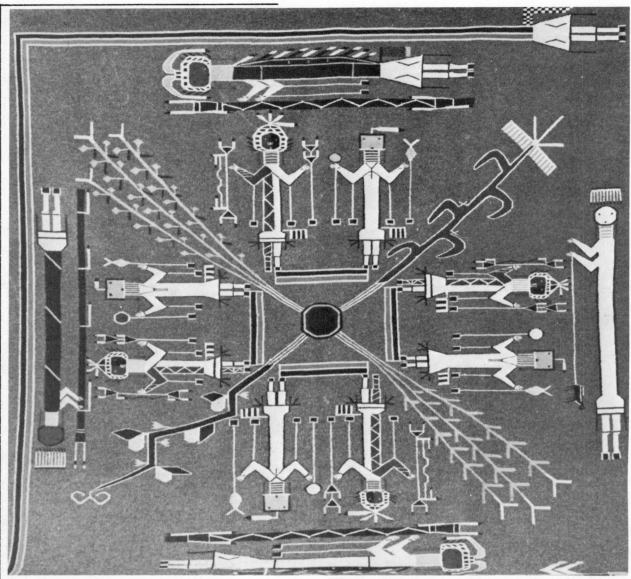

Part of a sandpainting design rug by Lola Yazzie won many first prize ribbons besides a Grand Award. Approximately 6' x 6', grey background.

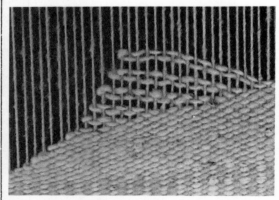

Photo N83. Weaving one area at a time forming a lazy line, Steps 1, 2 and 3

area. Where these two areas meet, there is a faint diagonal line called the lazy line. To join two areas correctly, proceed as follows:

Step 1—Starting with the right area, weave to the left a comfortable distance and bring your weft to the front. Change shed and weave back to right edge.

Step 2—Weave to the left but stop one warp thread to the right of the one you just turned on. Change shed and weave back to the right.

Step 3—Continue as above but turn on succeeding warp threads to the right as you weave, forming a diagonal line. (See photo N83.) Weave as high as you wish but probably no more than 9" or 10".

Step 4—Weave to the left and let the weft follow the diagonal line down to the woven web on the left side and weave out to the left edge. (See photo N84.) Change shed.

Step 5—Weave to right stopping at the first warp thread that you turned on when beginning right area. Change shed and weave back reversing on the same warp thread.

Step 6—Continue weaving, reversing weft on succeeding warp threads to the right. When you have reached the top of the diagonal the web will be level with first woven area. (See photos N85 and N86.) Some of the Navajo weavers do not use this weft yarn following down the diagonal line. It is not especially found in the older rugs. The weaver weaves the diagonal line as detailed here and then adds a new weft at the beginning of the new area to be woven.

To join areas without a lazy line—I've seen some weavers join two areas without any sign of the joining. For this method proceed as follows:

Step 1—Beginning with the left area, weave to the right a comfortable distance and bring weft to surface of weaving.

Step 2—Change shed and weave back to left but leave a loop of weft about 2″ to 3″ long at right.

Step 3—Change sheds and weave back to right stopping one warp thread to left of previous weft.

Step 4—Change shed and weave back to left leaving a loop of weft on right.

Step 5—Continue for as high as you wish but no more than 9″ to 10″. (See photo N87.)

Step 6—Now weave the right area as follows: Open to next shed, break first loop of weft (do not cut) and weave to right with the lowest short end. With new weft, overlap and weave on across to right edge. Change shed. (See photo N88.)

Step 7—Weave back to left and stop weft just before woven area at left. Overlap the corresponding short end from left area.

Step 8—Continue breaking loops and overlapping with weft of right area until second area is level with first. Zigzag the actual splice area as much as possible. No lazy line shows with this method.

Raised Outline Technique

The raised outline is a recent innovation in Navajo weaving. (See page 3 of color section for weave detail.) You usually find this type of rug being woven in the Tuba City-Coal Mine Mesa area. This is not a difficult weave but it takes close watching to do it correctly. I find two ways of doing this weave. One is to carry one color of weft all the way across and let the outline be formed by a second color. The other way, the one we have described here, uses two colors for each area, both

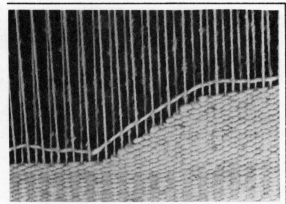

Photo N84. Lazy Line, Step 4

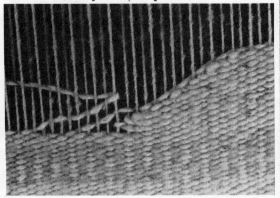

Photo N85. Lazy Line, Steps 5 and 6

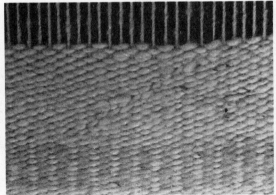

Photo N86. The lazy line where two areas join is barely visible.

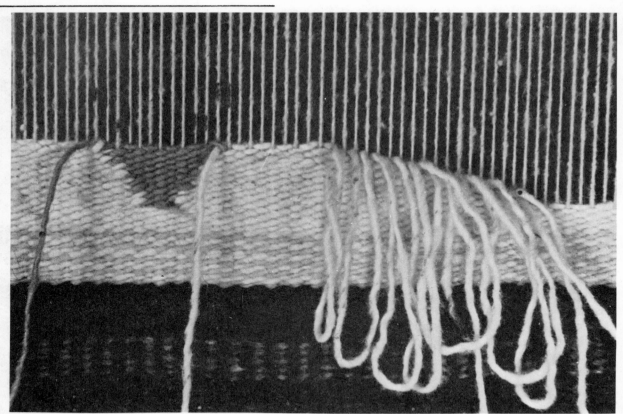

Photo N87. Joining two areas *without* a lazy line showing. Steps 1, 2, 3, 4 and 5.

Photo N88. Overlapping the wefts of two adjacent areas, Step 6.

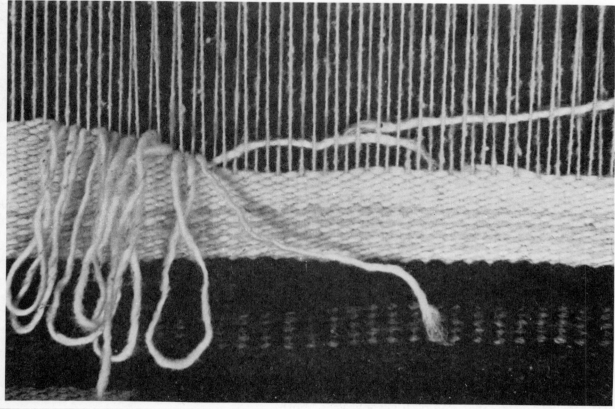

forming the outline. This is the most difficult. If you can do this one, you can do the other one. The raised outline is always woven with two colors so I would suggest that you begin with a stripe using two colors before you try a design effect.

Be sure your weft yarns are the same thickness because you cannot correct and fill in when you are working a one and one color arrangement or it will show drastically.

Get used to the idea that you use a stick shed for color one and the pull shed for color two and this does not change. Both colors must be woven in the same direction. Also treat your selvage the same for both colors. For example:

Row 1—Stick shed. Split selvage on left. Weave right to left with color one.

Row 2—Change to pull shed and split selvage on left again. Weave right to left with color two. Both wefts are on the left now.

Row 3—Change to stick shed and split selvage on right. Weave left to right with color one.

Row 4—Change to pull shed and split selvage on right again. Weave left to right with color two. Both wefts are on the right again. Continue in this one and one color arrangement until you thoroughly understand it. It produces a vertical effect in the weave.

Regarding these directions for weaving the selvage, I experimented and decided this way gives you the neatest selvage for this type of weaving.

Up until a few weeks ago I would have said that the raised outline was always used in diagonal pattern lines. However, at the most recent Navajo show at the Museum of Northern Arizona in Flagstaff I saw a rug that had some kind of a raised outline effect in the vertical lines. We will discuss the raised outline on the diagonal as this is the most common.

When you feel confident weaving the one and one color arrangement, you are ready to begin a definite design. To understand what you want to achieve, read the following carefully.

As you already have learned you get a diagonal line by turning wefts on adjoining warp threads. Refer to directions for weaving the flat diamond (page 58). In the raised outline technique you are doing the same thing but using two colors and this automatically gives you a skipped effect. Let us say you are going to make a diagonal line beginning on the tenth and ending on the thirtieth warp thread. You would turn color one weft on the tenth warp. You would turn color two weft on the eleventh warp, turn color one weft on the twelfth warp, turn color two weft on the thirteenth warp, etc. You can see for color one to turn on the tenth warp and the twelfth that it must skip over the eleventh warp, and for color two to turn on the eleventh and thirteenth warp it must skip over the twelfth warp. As the weft turns it covers the warp it reverses on as well as the adjacent one on the back shed thus giving the appearance of a two thread skip and forming a raised outline.

You may find it difficult to remember which shed to use next so think of it this way: You know you have to weave a pair of wefts in the same direction, so just remember that when both wefts are together on the same side, you use the stick shed and when the wefts are divided you use the pull shed. (It doesn't actually make any difference which shed you begin with. Just don't change the sequence once you begin.)

When the two wefts, color one and two, are hanging together at the diagonal line always pick up the one to weave from below. The wefts never interlock with each other in any way. If you lift the other weft up out of the way before you pick up the one you want to weave with, you should have it right.

To help you get started, here are some detailed instructions. Let's assume you are weaving a triangular design in the middle giving you three areas to weave.

Row 1—Stick shed. Split left selvage. With C1–A1 (color one, area one) weave right to left toward the center and stop where A2 (area two) begins. On the very next warp thread which is on the back of the shed, fasten in C1–A2. Weave across to the beginning of A3. On the very next warp thread, fasten in C1–A3 and weave to left edge.

Row 2—Pull shed. Split left selvage. Beginning on right fasten in C2–A1 and weave one warp thread beyond C1–A1. On the very next warp thread fasten in C2–A2 and weave across A2 stopping one warp thread to the right of C1–A2. On the very next warp thread fasten in C2–A3 and weave to left edge. There is now one warp thread between C1 and C2 and A1 and A2. All wefts are now on left of each area so we begin weaving with weft on right or C1–A1.

Row 3—Stick shed. Split right selvage. Pick up C1–A1 and weave to right edge. In so doing, you make it turn around one warp and go in front of this warp and the adjacent warp on the back shed. C1 is actually covering two warp threads at this point before it goes into shed. We now want to weave C1–A2. Hold C2–A2 up out of the way and pick up C1 from underneath and weave to right, as explained above. It comes out of the shed at same place as C2–A1 is hanging. Weave C1–A3 by taking it into shed and coming out at same place as C2–A2.

You now have c1–a1 hanging on right, c2–a1 and c1–a2 hanging at right of a2. You have c2–a2 and c1–a3 hanging at left of a2 and the two wefts of each pair are hanging between the same warp threads. c2–a3 is on the left.

Row 4—Pull shed and split right selvage. Weave c2–a1 to right edge. Weave c2–a2 and come out of shed one warp thread to left of c1. Weave c2–a3 and come out of shed one warp thread beyond c1–a3. All wefts are on right and the pairs of wefts of a2 and a3 are hanging with one warp end between.

Row 5—Weave c1–a3. (See photo N89,

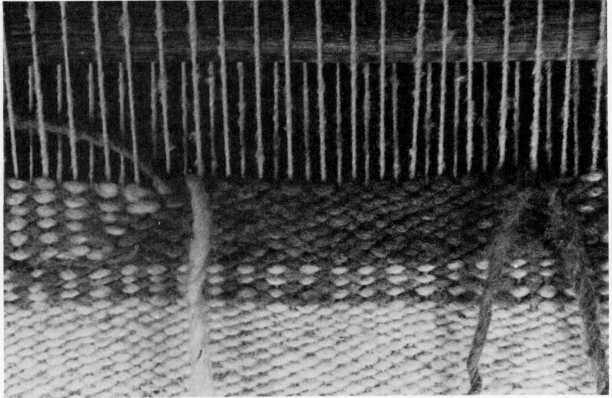

Photo N89. Raised Outline—right, at end of Row 4, one warp between c1 and c2, a2; left, beginning of Row 5 c1, a3 woven.

taken at this point.) Weave c1–a2 and come out between same warp as c2–a3. Weave c1–a1 and come out between same warps as c2–a2.

Row 6—Weave c2–a3. Weave c2–a2 and come out one warp thread to right of c1–a2. Weave c2–a1 and come out one warp beyond c1–a1. Continue as established.

Note: In the beginning, for one time only because of fastening in your wefts, you do not get the skip effect at right side of a2 until you are in the fifth row. Also for one time only at this point c1 turns on same warp as you fastened c2.

Four Heddle Weaving

Some Navajos learn to weave more intricate patterns by using more than two shed sticks. We cannot dwell at length on this type of weaving but we will give you one setup so you will have some knowledge of it. If you do not understand four harness weaving then a lesson in basic draft writing would be helpful at this time. See references in Appendix for information on draft writing.

Up until now you have been weaving a plain weave type fabric—over one, under one, over, under, etc. With four shed sticks your weft works through the fabric with more variation. The weft will skip over more than one warp at a time. Also the order in which you use the shed sticks will vary the weave.

We will give you details on a double-faced weave, one of the simplest setups of four heddle weaving. With this setup each side will be different. For example: You can weave a design fabric on the front and a one color fabric on the back, or a design fabric on the front and a one and one color arrangement on the back.

The Navajo would not record the directions the way we will give it to you but I feel this method will make it easy for you to understand.

A—Showing which warp threads each shed stick controls. You have one stick shed, line 4, and three pull sheds, lines 3, 2 and 1.

Note that heddle stick two is an exact opposite of heddle stick four. Heddle stick one is opposite to heddle stick three. That is: What you didn't pick up on four you put in a heddle on two and what you didn't heddle on three, you put in a heddle on one. You will use heddle sticks three and four to weave the back and heddle sticks one and two to weave the front.

B—Heddle arrangement. Circled numbers denote number and order of warp threads that should be brought forward to form sheds.

Set up your warp with twice as many warp threads per inch, about sixteen depending on size of weft yarns, then proceed as follows:

Step 1—Prepare heddle stick four first. This is the stick shed. Refer to diagram N7b and follow line 4. Pick up all circled numbers on heddle stick; that is, reading from right to left skip one warp,

Diagram N7.

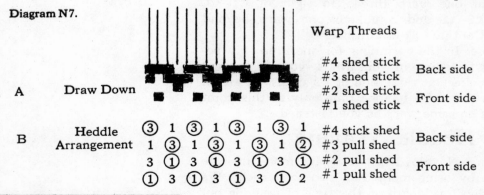

		Warp Threads
		#4 shed stick — Back side
		#3 shed stick
A	Draw Down	#2 shed stick — Front side
		#1 shed stick

B	Heddle Arrangement	③ 1 ③ 1 ③ 1 ③ 1	#4 stick shed — Back side
		1 ③ 1 ③ 1 ③ 1 ②	#3 pull shed
		3 ① 3 ① 3 ① 3 ①	#2 pull shed — Front side
		① 3 ① 3 ① 3 ① 2	#1 pull shed

pick up three warps, skip one, pick up three, skip one, pick up three, etc., across the warp. Check it and when correct, push heddle stick four to top of warp.

Step 2—Prepare pull shed three. With heddle stick pick up two warps, skip one, pick up three, skip one, pick up three, skip one, etc., across the warp. Note that the one you skip is always the middle one of the three you picked up on four. Check and push stick to top of warp.

Step 3—Prepare pull shed two. With heddle stick pick up one, skip three, pick up one, skip three, etc., across warp. You will notice that this is the exact opposite of stick four. Check and push stick to top of warp.

Step 4—Prepare pull shed one and with *batten* skip two, pick up one, skip three, pick up one, etc., across the warp. You will notice that this is the exact opposite of heddle stick three. Check for accuracy.

Step 5—Turn batten horizontally and with heddle stick and heddle cord make heddles around all warps on front of batten. Check and push to bottom of warp.

Step 6—Insert batten in opening made by stick two and take out heddle stick. Turn batten horizontally and make heddles around all warps on front of batten. Be sure heddles are not too short for sticks two and three because in using these sticks the shed is made through the heddles below it. Push stick to bottom of warp.

Step 7—Insert batten and take out heddle stick three. Turn batten horizontally and make heddles around all warps on front of batten. You make only *one* heddle around each group of three warps. There is no need to make a heddle around each individual warp thread since the three warp threads are all adjacent to each other with no warps in between.

Step 8—Heddle stick four remains as is. Double check to be sure you have made no errors. (See photos N90 and N91.)

Photo N90. Four-heddle weaving, Step 7— You make one heddle around three warp threads on heddle stick three.

Photo N91. Four-heddle loom—heddle stick one at bottom, four at top.

You are now ready to weave. Weave first four rows as given in earlier chapter. Be sure yarns for front and back of your fabric are the same weight and twist so they build up the same in the weaving. Use heddle sticks one and two (two lower ones) and weave front design. Use heddle sticks three and four (two upper ones) and weave back design. Repeat this one-two-three-four order throughout.

It is difficult to keep the back color from showing on the front and vice versa. Get lots of weft in the shed so yarn can puff out and cover. (See photo N92.)

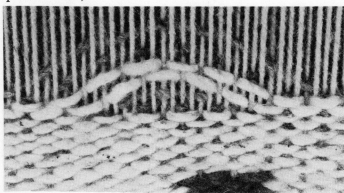

Photo N92. Four wefts showing—two white on front fabric and two grey on back fabric.

Source of Supplies

Navajo-type looms
Living Designs
313 South Murphy Avenue
Sunnyvale, California 94086

The Pendleton Shop
P.O. Box 233, Jordan Road
Sedona, Arizona 86336

Battens and combs (forks)
Gillans's Specialties
P.O. Box 633
Solana Beach, California 92075

Living Designs

The Pendleton Shop

Occasionally can be found at trading posts on the reservation.

Bag or sack needles
The Pendleton Shop

Warp and weft yarns
Carmel Valley Handweavers Supply
1342 Camino Del Mar
Del Mar, California 92014

Casa de Los Tejedoras
1619 E. Edinger
Santa Ana, California 92705

Dharma Trading Co.
P.O. Box 1288
Berkeley, California 94701

Folklorico
P.O. Box 625
Palo Alto, California 94302

The Pendleton Shop
(Navajo handspun yarns from the reservation)

Robin and Russ Handweavers
533 North Adams St.
McMinnville, Oregon 97128

Tahki Imports Ltd.
336 West End Avenue
New York, New York 10023

Yarn Primitives
P.O. Box 1013
Weston, Connecticut 06880

Mrs. Paula Simmons
Box 12
Suquamish, Washington 98392
(Yarns spun to order)

Fleece for spinning
The Freed Co.
P.O. Box 394
Albuquerque, New Mexico 47103

Greentree Ranch
Rt. 3, Box 461
Loveland, Colorado 80537

Hand cards for carding wool
The Freed Co.

Greentree Ranch

The Pendleton Shop

Robin and Russ Handweavers

Spincraft
Box 332
Richardson, Texas 75080

Spindles—Navajo type
Living Designs

The Pendleton Shop

Schacht Spindle Co.
1708 Walnut St.
Boulder, Colorado 80302

Dye materials
Dharma Trading Co.

Books on Navajo weaving
Craft & Hobby Book Service
P.O. Box 626
Pacific Grove, California 93950

The Pendleton Shop

Robin and Russ Handweavers

Further Reading

Dye Plants and Dyeing by the Brooklyn Botanic Garden (Brooklyn, N.Y.: Brooklyn Botanic Garden, 1964).

Handspinning by Allen Fannin (New York: Litton Publishing Co., 1970).

Indian Arts by Andrew H. Whiteford (New York: Golden Press, 1970).

Lichens for Vegetable Dyeing by Eileen Bolton (London: Studio Vista Publishers, 1972).

The Looming Arts by Mary Pendleton, Vol. 4 No. 4 (1969) to Vol. 6 No. 3 (1971). Published by Mary Pendleton, Sedona, Arizona.

The Navajo by Clyde Kluckhahn and Dorothea Leighton (Garden City, N.Y.: Doubleday Anchor Book, 1962).

Navajo Native Dyes by Nonabah Bryan and Stella Young (Lawrence, Kan.: Haskell Institute, 1940).

Navajo Rugs by Gilbert S. Maxwell (Palm Desert, Calif.: Best-West Publications, 1963).

Navajo Shepherd and Weaver by Gladys A. Reichard (Glorieta, N.M.: Rio Grande Press, 1934).

Navajo Weavers & Silversmiths by Dr. Washington Matthews (Palmer Lake, Colo.: Filter Press, 1968).

Navaho Weaving by Charles A. Amsden (Glorieta, N.M.: Rio Grande Press, 1934).

Navajo Weaving Today by Bertha P. Dutton (Sante Fe, N.M.: Museum of New Mexico Press, 1961).

Pueblo Crafts by Ruth Underhill (Lawrence, Kan.: Haskell Institute, 1944).

The Shuttlecraft Book of American Handweaving by Mary Meigs Atwater (New York: Macmillan Publishing Co., 1928), for draft writing.

Spider Woman by Gladys A. Reichard (Glorieta, N.M.: Rio Grande Press, 1934).

The Story of Navajo Weaving by Kate Peck Kent (Phoenix, Ariz.: Heard Museum of Anthropology and Primitive Arts, 1961).

Vegetable Dyeing by Alma Lesch (New York: Watson-Guptill Publishing Co., 1970).

Weavers Book by Harriet Tidball (New York: Macmillan Publishing Co., 1961), for draft writing.

Working With Wool by Noel Bennett and Tiana Bighorse (Flagstaff, Ariz.: Northland Press, 1971).

Your Handspinning by Elsie G. Davenport (Pacific Grove, Calif.: Craft & Hobby Book Service, 1964).

Index

Woven woolen blanket,
Navajo, Arizona. (Courtesy
Museum of the American
Indian, Heye Foundation.)

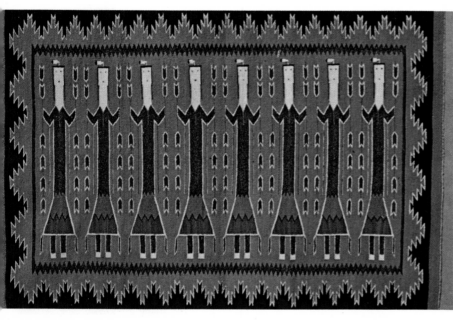

Yeibichai by K. Noe.
First Prize ribbon,
approximately 4' x 5'.

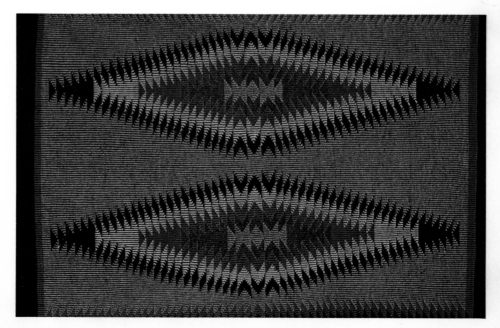

Raised outline rug by
Ruth Hatathli.
First Prize Inter-tribal
Ceremonial 1971.

Chief Blanket design—No matter how you fold it, the design is balanced. Top by Grace Brown, folded in foreground by Bertha Harvey.

Top left, double-face rug by Marie Begay; top right, double-face rug by Edith James; bottom, twill weave rug by Bah Hatathli. Best in the Class First Prize ribbon 1971 Inter-tribal Ceremonial, approximately 6' x 8'.

Left, Ganado Red by Mary
Toadachinny; top right, Vegetable
dye by Blanche Hale; bottom right,
by Alice James.

Background rug, crystal rug by Mary
Moore; top right, by Alice Smith;
bottom left, by Mary Ann Roan;
bottom right, double-face rug, weaver
unidentified.

Two Grey Hills by Mary Tsosie.

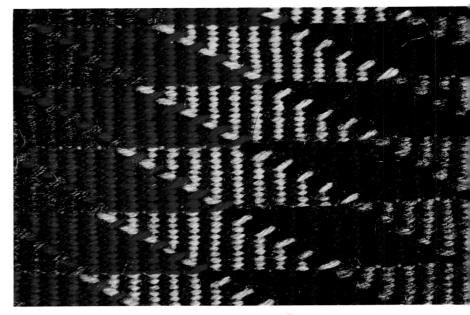

Detail of raised outline rug.

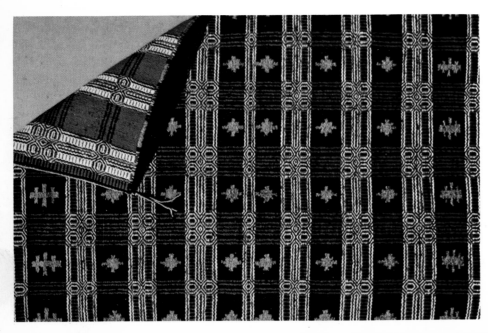

Double-face rug
by Edith James.

Woven and embroidered anklets, Hopi, Arizona. (Courtesy Museum of the American Indian, Heye Foundation.)

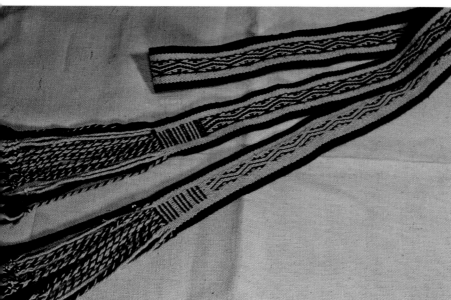

Hopi woven belt, width 2½″, length 88″ with 10″ fringe. Brown and off-white wool. (Courtesy of the Museum of Northern Arizona)

Embroidered dance sash, Hopi, Arizona. (Courtesy Museum of the American Indian, Heye Foundation.)

Hopi woven sash by Keevema of Hoteville, 1941. Narrow white band on bottom is woven with cotton. The large upper white area woven with wool. Every ninth and tenth warp loop is knotted in a square knot for finish of fringe. The warp is an extra heavy four-ply cotton. Selvage and top twining cord are respun knitting worsted. Width varies from 10½″ to 11½″. Length is about 42″ per piece plus 3¾″ fringe. Note reverse side of pattern area. (Courtesy of the Museum of Northern Arizona)

Sampler hanging by Pauline Trask in embroidery weave technique.

An Anglo weaver's use of the embroidery weave technique: "Oriental Dance" by Pauline Trask.

Hopi woven sash by Lolamayoma of Shungopovi, 1925. Warp is three-ply lightweight cotton. The selvage and twining cord is a coarse wool. To finish fringe every pair of warp loops is knotted together. The added red felt piece has a ceremonial significance. Width varies from 9½" to 10½". Each piece is 41¾" long, fringe is 3". Note reverse side. (Courtesy of the Museum of Northern Arizona)

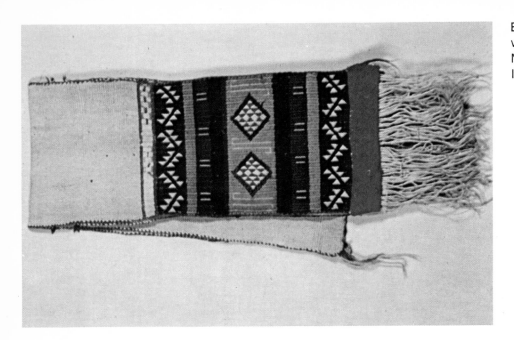

Embroidered dance sash with red trim. (Courtesy Museum of the American Indian, Heye Foundation.)

Willie Sitzwiisah Coin, Hopi weaver, with one of his Hopi belts.

Hopi woven belt, width 2″, length 32″ with 13″ fringe. Red, green and black wool. (Courtesy of the Museum of Northern Arizona)

HOPI
TECHNIQUES

Contents

Introduction

Mary Pendleton, a master weaver and craftswoman, has always admired the weaving of the Hopi people. It is a joy to add a few words regarding my people and their weaving to this book which lends inspiration to those who are already weavers and to those who wish to enjoy this profession.

The Hopi people have been weavers for many centuries, being skilled in using cotton which was brought from the south during the time of their migration. Natural vegetation was used also in the weaving of baskets.

Cotton was used for ceremonial dress and for clothing as well as for wedding capes and for blankets.

Weaving of the ceremonial costumes, clothing and blankets was and still is, woven by the men of the tribe. Baskets, by the women. The same method is used today as in ancient times. The loom, in ancient times, was tied to the trunk of a tree and around the weaver's body.

The ceremonial sash, wedding belt, woman's black dress and blanket designs are woven into the cloth. The ceremonial kilt design is embroidered with a needle on the woven fabric at each end. The ceremonial kilt is used only in special ceremonies. Usually you see the sash being worn. Wedding capes are the largest of the woven articles.

The ceremonial woman's belt is also used by men at times of ceremony. In ancient days the cotton was dyed from natural vegetation and mineral red, green and black. Today colored wool yarn is used.

The white design on the woman's wedding belt within the other colors represents the planetary life, and when worn by the female around her waist, is in keeping with the thought of her bringing in new life.

The ceremonial sash is worn by the men only in religious ceremonials. Woven of white cotton with each end interwoven in designs of red, green and black on the white background, it represents the universe and the blessings of divine power and the heavens.

A very important blanket is woven for the child before he is born. It is known to the Hopi as a magic blanket or *Qwa-quil-ho-ya* in Hopi, which means step beyond. It is of square design in black and white, has a deep spiritual meaning and each boy and girl must have one. The design differs somewhat in each.

If the child passes on, he is always wrapped in this blanket to take him "one step beyond." Today this blanket has been found in ancient ruins.

Each stitch and every design and color has a deep meaning to the Hopi, all inclusive and all in relation to the Creator and the heavens and the earth, the universe as a whole.

It is in appreciation to Mary Pendleton for this interesting and very informative book and her wonderful knowledge of weaving that I say: *kwakwai* (thank you.).

White Bear Fredericks
Member of Coyote Clan
meaning Protector of the Ritual

White Bear Fredericks, Hopi

The Warp Float Weave—Belt

The Hopi are a small tribe of Indians living in northeast Arizona. Their reservation is surrounded by the Navajo reservation. The Hopis regard themselves as the first inhabitants of America. Their village of Oraibi is the oldest continuously occupied settlement in the United States. Hopi is pronounced Hō pē.

The word Hopi means peace. The Hopi people have always been peaceful people devoting their efforts to farming and various crafts including pottery, basketry, weaving, silverwork and painting. The Hopi men do the weaving but there are few today who are actively engaged in this craft. The Hopi men weave blankets, belts, garters, headbands and sashes used in their ceremonies.

Their blankets are woven on a primitive, upright loom and in a manner much like the Navajo rug weaving described elsewhere in this book but we will cover two other types of Hopi weaving, the warp float weave used for narrow belts and bands and the embroidery weave used in the man's ceremonial sash.

Working with the Indian one is always aware that it is difficult for them to explain why they do things a certain way. They have learned a particular way, they know what they want to happen and they just begin to weave. One can sit and observe for many hours and still miss some of the finer points of what they are doing.

I found out from observation and discussions with the Hopi weavers that they do not always do things the same way. For instance, they usually prefer to have an even number of threads in the side stripe area, but if they run short of yarn, they may very well have an odd number of threads. If they miscalculate in winding the warp, they just adjust the pick-up sequence to suit the warp as it turns out. One thread difference on one side or the other doesn't bother them.

I began weaving a Hopi belt in a method that I had observed. After I got started, one of the Hopi weavers said he preferred to begin winding his warp on the left. This puts one extra warp color on the right rather than on the left. However, when he sat down to my warp he said "This is fine," and he simply adjusted his sequence of pick-up and began to weave. As with many things you can arrive at the same goal from different avenues. The important thing is that you learn the technique—it's the same whether you begin on the right or left in winding the warp.

Having worked with students learning this belt weave, I know that it can be confusing and so

I chose a procedure that is the simplest to explain. When you have made your sample and are familiar with the basic weave construction, you will find it easy to decide on any color arrangement or number of warps and still do the weave. You will know how to adjust just as the Hopi weaver does.

Many weavers look at a Hopi belt and dismiss it lightly as just inkle weaving which they consider a very simple weave. Yes, some inkle type weaves are very basic and simple but then there are some that take much thought and concentration. The Hopi belt weave with the pattern in reverse on the back side is one of these. Do not dismiss this weave as just another inkle weave. It is a real challenge.

Materials and Tools Needed for Your Hopi Belt Loom

Large loom rods—three large dowels 1″ to 2″ in diameter, 18″ to 24″ long. A good substitute for dowels would be broom handles or straight tree limbs.

Two smaller loom rods and a shed stick—three dowels ¾″ to 1″ in diameter, 14″ to 18″ long.

Heddle stick—one dowel ⅜″ diameter, about 16″ long.

Batten/beater—at least 10″ long and about 1½″ wide. (See diagram N1, Navajo section for details on making batten.)

Pointed stick—⅜″ dowel, 10″ to 12″ long. Use pencil sharpener to make the point on one end and sand smooth.

Photo H1. Materials needed for Hopi belt loom weaving. Top to bottom: 3 large loom rods, 2 smaller loom rods, shed stick, heddle stick, shuttle, pointed stick, two types of batten/beaters, 3 balls of respun wool yarn, heavy cord, cone of heddle string.

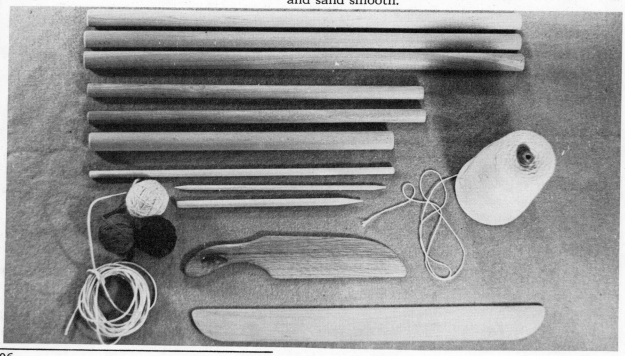

Shuttle—$\frac{3}{16}$" to $\frac{1}{4}$" dowel about 10" long with both ends pointed.

Heavy rope or doubled harness cord.

Heavy cotton cord for making heddles. About 8 yards and at least six-ply. (See photo H1.)

Warping Frame

Materials needed: two pieces $\frac{3}{4}$" pine, 8" to 10" wide, 36" to 60" long, drilled as shown in photo H2. The holes are to be the same size as your largest loom rods. The rods must fit tightly in the holes. Holes are spaced for different length warps. As shown: 30"—36"—48"—54".

The warping frame can really be made in several ways but we illustrate on a frame similar to the one our Hopi instructor uses.

We are using two pieces for the frame. In the past the Hopi would make two holes in a wall of his house to hold the loom rods for one side and then have a board or equivalent to hold rods on the other side. We suggest that you place one side of your frame next to a wall to hold it steady and place blocks to hold other side in place. This would be the easiest way to simulate the Hopi warping frame. (See photo H2.)

Assembling the Warping Frame

Place section one of your warping frame against a wall. Place large dowel rod A in the end

Photo H2. Warping frame assembled ready for use. Note cement blocks inside and outside to hold frame side in place.

Photo H3. Use rubber bands or string around rods if holes are too big for rods.

Photo H4. Step 1, Respinning Yarn—Roll spindle away from you.

hole. Place large dowel rod B in one of the other holes depending on how long a belt you wish to weave. If the rods are 30″ apart, you will have a 60″ warp—actually a little less than 60″ as the wool stretches when you wind it and contracts when tension is off. We will place our rods 36″ apart for a 72″ warp. These two dowel rods are used as a part of the warping frame and then become a part of the loom.

Place section two of frame in place with ends of rods in corresponding holes. If rods slip in holes, place heavy string or rubber bands around rods. (See photo H3.) Place a cement block or some heavy object on the inside and one on the outside of section two of frame to hold it steady. (See photo H2.)

For comfort, place a footstool next to the outside section of your frame. Sit on stool and put feet inside of frame. Some of you may wish to place your warping frame on a table so you can stand to wind your warp.

Yarn

Warp

The warp must be very strong and smooth. This is a closely set warp and you would have difficulty with a fuzzy yarn. You should use a tightly twisted wool yarn. You can handspin it or do as the Hopi weavers do today, use four-ply knitting worsted, respun to make it smooth and strong.

Respinning Four-Ply Knitting Worsted for Warp—You might find it easier to respin your yarn on a spinning wheel. If so, just rotate the wheel counterclockwise to do it. The Hopi weaver uses a spindle to respin his yarn. The size of spindle might vary but a typical one would be light in weight, about 20″ total length with about 7″ below the whorl and the whorl about 3½″ in diameter.

To respin the Hopi way, sit on a chair with plenty of space around you. Tie a slip knot in end of yarn and slip over short end of spindle shaft below the whorl. You will do your spinning on the short end of the spindle. Lay your skein of knitting worsted on floor to left of you. Place spindle across your right thigh with whorl end pointing to left. With yarn in left hand, hold it about a half yard above end of spindle.

Step 1—With spindle shaft close to your body, place right palm down with end of fingers on shaft and push forward and away from you. The spindle will turn as you move your hand and yarn will wind around the end of the spindle. (See photo H4.)

Step 2—Cup your fingers a little and pull

shaft back toward you but do not let it *roll* back or you will *un*wind your yarn. (See photo H5.)

Step 3—Move your right hand forward again with a fast rubbing motion while lifting your hand so the spindle can continue to turn. It should keep turning even when your curved fingers are drawing it back toward you. You want a constant rotation of the spindle while you are moving it forward and pulling it back. A little practice will develop your rhythm. The spindle is hanging from the yarn and swinging back and forth a little as you twirl it. The yarn between your left hand and end of spindle gets shorter as you twist it and there is a snapping sound as it tightens up and slips off the point of the spindle shaft.

Step 4—When all the yarn has been twisted and the twists have curled up at the point and your left hand is only a few inches away from spindle point (see photo H6), lay spindle on the floor with the short end away from you. In so doing more yarn will draw into your left hand from the skein. Now put your right foot on the long end of spindle to hold it steady.

Step 5—Stretch the yarn up and out with your left hand and beginning at the spindle shaft on the floor run the fingers of your right hand up the yarn to the left hand forcing and spreading the twist evenly along the yarn. Do this several times. (See photo H7.)

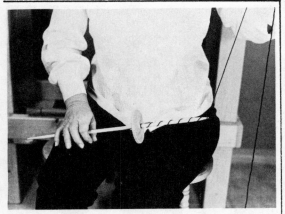

Photo H5. Step 2—Cup fingers of right hand and draw spindle toward you.

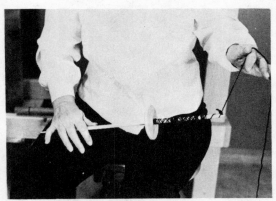

Photo H6. Step 4—All yarn drawn out has been tightly spun and it curls up at point of spindle.

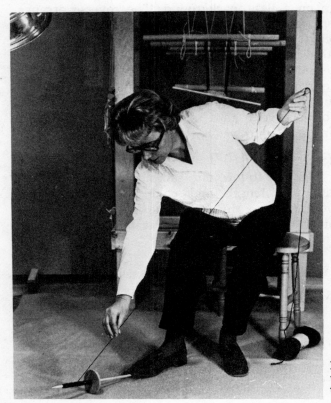

Photo H7. Step 5—Holding spindle steady with right foot, fingers of right hand force twist evenly up yarn.

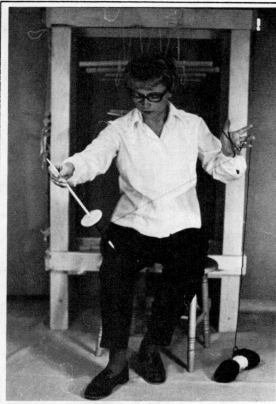

Photo H8. Step 7—Winding yarn onto short end of spindle shaft.

Photo H9. Step 8—Cradle spindle between feet and wind yarn into tight ball.

Step 6—Wrap yarn around thumb and little finger of left hand to keep tension until you can pick up the spindle from floor with right hand.

Step 7—Wind respun yarn onto short end of spindle and repeat from Step 1. (See photo H8.)

Step 8—When you have a quantity respun, cradle your spindle between your feet with the whorl resting at your ankles and short end pointing ahead of you. Wind yarn into a tight ball. As you pull the yarn, the spindle will turn. (See photo H9.) Put a lot of twist in the yarn so it kinks quite a bit when relaxed.

Weft

The Hopi weavers use a cotton yarn for weft. It usually is a medium weight two-ply cotton about the weight of a 5/2 yarn. The weft should be the same color as the edge warp threads.

Color Selection of Yarn

My color selection is not typically Hopi. I have picked my colors for ease in seeing and photographing the yarns. The sample will be brown, rust and cream. However, those of you who want to do a typical Hopi color arrangement might use 16 black, 16 green, 16 red, 25 red and black alternated, 16 red, 16 green, 16 black. The warp would probably be arranged with the black of center section on top of shed stick and red in heddles. If you set it up this way, you will have a dark design on a light background. The reverse arrangement, which I chose, gives a light color on dark background. The sample will be a narrower belt with 4 brown, 4 rust, 4 cream, 21 brown and cream alternated, 4 cream, 4 rust, 4 brown. The back side of the belt is always a reverse coloring. When you choose your colors, keep in mind that dark colors are very hard to see and work with when doing a pick-up weave.

Amount of Yarn Needed

If you follow our sample as we give it in width and length and color arrangement, you should prepare the following amounts of respun four-ply knitting worsted for warp:

1½ to 2 oz. brown
1½ to 2 oz. cream
½ to ¾ oz. rust
About 40 yards of weft

About Design

The design for this type of weaving can be worked out on graph paper. Designs could be of small triangles in various shapes and arrangements, slanted lines or squares, just to suggest a few.

I was going to say that the stripes on the edge are always even numbered warp groups but then I looked at more belts from the museum and found that some have odd number of warp ends in the stripes. It appears that they can be any number, usually from four to sixteen warps of each color. The center area is usually an odd number of pairs of warps. For a wider belt use twenty-five pairs of warps with colors alternated. For a narrower belt use twenty-one pairs.

Winding the Warp

For our sample belt we will wind 4 ends brown, 4 ends rust, 4 ends cream, 21 brown and 21 cream alternated, 4 ends cream, 4 ends rust, 4 ends brown. Adjust instructions if your arrangement is different.

Step 1—Tie the brown yarn to rod A on right. Leave some space between tie and side of frame. Use a loose knot that can be untied later.

Step 2—Carry your ball of yarn to the left and take it over and under rod B. Carry yarn to right under and over rod A. Continue winding yarn in this manner. You do not have a cross as in other warping methods. You are going round and round. (See diagram H1.) Place yarn loops close

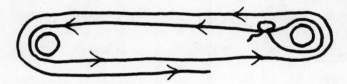

Diagram H1. Warp is wound round and round with no cross in the middle.

(MERVIN WOLFF)

together on rods. When you can count four loops on rod B, bring yarn back to rod A and cut.

The important thing is to have the same tension on all threads. Try not to make it tight or loose but arrive at a happy medium.

Step 3—Tie rust yarn to brown yarn making sure the knot is at rod A. (See photo H10.) Wind as directed until you can count four rust loops on rod B. End at rod A and cut. Run your hand between upper and lower part of warp to be sure no threads are crossed. Do this often to check.

Step 4—Tie cream yarn to rust yarn and wind until you have four loops on rod B. End at rod A. Up until now you have placed the loops close together on the rods. Beginning at this point you will space them more openly, about ¼" apart. (See photo H10.)

Photo H10. First 12 warp threads wound and a part of the center section. Notice spacing variation and knots at rod A.

Step 5—Continue winding with the cream yarn and spacing open until you have twenty-one loops on rod B. End at rod A. Secure the cream yarn to hold tension but do not cut or break it.

Step 6—Slip the end of the brown yarn under the first twelve warp threads you wound and pull it down to center of rod so the friction will hold it. Now wind the brown yarn and place it in the open spaces between the cream warp threads. (See photo H11.) Wind until you have twenty-one brown

Photo H11. Winding second color of center section.

loops on rod B. Bring brown yarn from last loop on rod B underneath and diagonally across to where you began brown yarn. Pull out the end caught under the first twelve warps and tie these two ends together. (See photo H12.) At this point note that the last loop on rod B is cream. This pairs with the last brown. You should have twenty-one pairs.

Step 7—Unfasten cream yarn and continue to wind until you have four more loops on rod B. Place them close together on the rods as in the beginning. By now you have noticed that you have five cream loops on rod B after the last brown loop. Don't be confused. This is correct. Remember, the one cream loop pairs with the brown. End on rod A and cut.

Step 8—Tie on rust yarn and wind until you have four loops on rod B. End on rod A and cut.

Step 9—Tie on brown yarn and wind until

you have four loops on rod B. End on rod A and cut leaving a rather long end. Tie around rod A with a loose loop that can be untied later. (See photo H12.)

Photo H12. Completed warp. Note center section with colors alternated and first and last brown thread tied together.

Note: Keep all knots at rod A and not in the middle of warp somewhere. If you come across a knot in your yarn, unwind to rod A, cut yarn and remove knot, tie at this point and continue.

When you cut your yarn, it will unwind very easily. Before tying on again, retwist yarn with your fingers.

Making the Cross

Step 1—Beginning on left with pointed stick, pick up the alternate threads of the top warp. Pick up first warp with point and transfer it to left hand. Pick up third, fifth, etc. You will be picking up the cream threads in the center section. (See photo H13.) Insert shed stick in this shed (opening made by pointed stick).

Step 2—Tie a string to the end of this stick, take string under all warp ends of *top* warp and tie to other end. This secures shed stick so it cannot fall out. Remove pointed stick. (See photo H14.) Push shed stick up out of the way.

Step 3—Begin on left and pick up with point of stick warp threads of top warp that you didn't pick up before. Transfer them to your left hand. Always put point of stick on dowel rod A where

Photo H13. Step 1, Making the Cross—Picking up every other thread with pointed stick for stick shed.

Photo H14. Step 2—Shed stick in place. Note string tie to prevent it from falling out of warp.

warp is spaced out to locate correct warp to be picked up. It's easy to cross threads so do this pick-up carefully. Keep left hand up on warp away from rod A. (See photo H15.)

Photo H15. Step 3—Making the second pick-up for pull or heddle shed.

In this photo shed stick and left hand have been brought close to pick-up area for ease in photographing but it will be easier to do the pick-up if shed stick is pushed up out of the way and left hand is away from rod A. When pick-up is complete, slip pointed stick under threads in left hand.

Step 4—Push shed stick and pointed stick together and check to see if cross is correct. Every other thread should come from under the shed stick and over pointed stick and vice versa. The brown threads in center section will be on top of the pointed stick. (See photo H16.)

Step 5—Insert a loom rod in shed and remove pointed stick.

Making the Heddles

It is now necessary to make the heddles of your loom.

Step 1—Place cone of heavy cotton cord on the right and make a loop with slip knot in the end.

Step 2—Take this end of yarn from right to left through the shed made by the loom rod. Slip the loop over end of heddle stick but do not pull

Photo H16. Push sticks together to check for errors in pick up.

knot too tight. Holding the heddle stick in your left hand several inches away from the warp, reach between the first and second warp threads with your right index finger and thumb and grasp heddle string. Pull string up out of warp. Twist string to the right and put over end of stick. (See photo H17.) Grasp this same yarn and twist to left and put over end of stick. (See photo H18.) Adjust

Photo H17. Step 2, Making Heddles—Twist right . . .

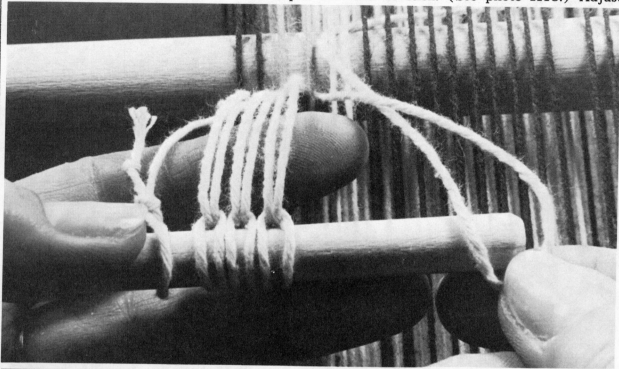

Photo H18. . . . then twist left.

length. Heddle is complete. Continue across making a heddle around each warp thread on top of loom rod. Heddles should be 2″ to 3″ long. Each heddle must be the same length or you will have difficulty in weaving. When all heddles are made, check to be sure you haven't missed a warp thread or that you haven't put two threads in one heddle.

Step 3—Push heddles together on heddle stick and make a half-hitch knot over end of stick with heddle string. Take string over heddles to left and do another half hitch at other end. Bring string back over heddles and fasten securely on right. This keeps heddles from separating on stick while you are weaving. (See photo H19.)

Step 4—Remove loom rod. You now have the shed stick above and the heddle stick below.

Removing Warp from Warping Frame

At top of warp make a cross using both top and bottom layers of warp.

Step 1—Pick up a group of four to eight warp ends from bottom warp, then four to eight ends from top warp, etc., across the warp. Insert one of the smaller loom rods in the opening made. A cross with grouped warps is made between rod B and this smaller rod.

Step 2—Take another loom rod the same size and lay it between upper and lower warp next to rod A at bottom of frame. Push this rod to top.

Photo H19. Step 3—Heddles fastened together for weaving.

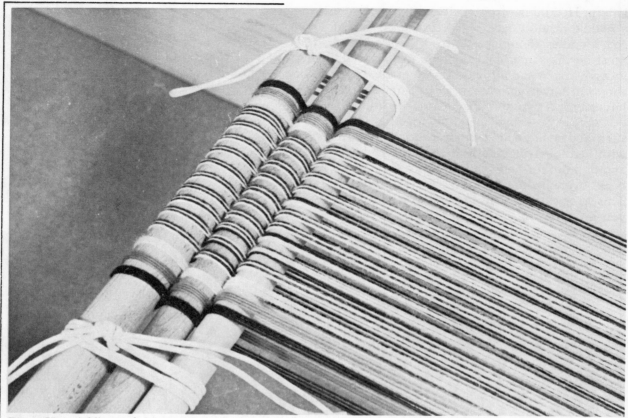

Photo H20. Adding rods at top of warp.

This separates the upper and lower warp again.

Step 3—Tie the three rods at top together. (See photo H20.)

Step 4—Release rod B from warping frame by pushing side sections apart a little. Roll warp to rod A and tie all rods together on each side of warp. Remove rod A and completed warp from warping frame. (See photo H21.)

Mounting Warp Ready for Weaving

At this point you must decide where you will mount your Hopi-type loom. It must be fastened at top and bottom to something solid. The Hopi weavers usually mount their looms to the floor and ceiling of their homes, You could put two large screw eyes, big enough to take the largest dowel rods, in the floor and put two in the ceiling with a rod between. It could be mounted in a sturdy frame or in an upright tapestry loom. We'll give directions for mounting our loom in a large frame.

Photo H21. Warp rolled, tied and removed from warping frame.

Step 1—Tie rod A (last one you took out of warping frame) to lower part of frame so that top warp with heddle stick will be in front when unrolled. Tie each side with heavy cord leaving a little space between rod A and frame.

Step 2—Lace heavy cord around top of frame and insert large loom rod C. The cord must go round and round and not cross between rod and frame. Rod C should hang low enough so space

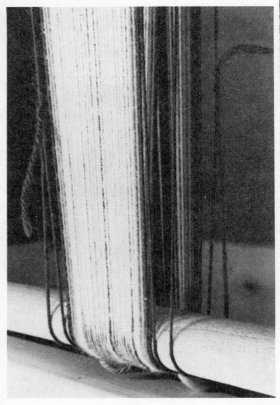

Photo H22. Rolled warp tied to bottom of loom frame and rod C hung from top of frame.

Photo H23. Retie ends of warp so there are no loops around rod A.

between rod A and C is less than length of warp. (See photo H22.)

Step 3—Unroll warp and tie rod B to rod C.

Step 4—Tighten tension by adjusting heavy cord between rod C and top of frame. (See Tensioning of Warp, page 40.) Tension of warp must be tight but not as tight as for Navajo rug weaving.

Step 5—Push warp together on rod A.

Step 6—Untie loop of first warp on right, take it front to back under rod A and tie to first warp on back. Use an overhand knot, pull it tight around warp thread and slip it up to adjust tension. Untie loop on left and bring warp thread from back to front under rod A and tie to first warp on front. Now no warp crosses over top of rod A. (See photo H23.) This is necessary so you can move your warp as you weave.

Step 7—Tie a string across warp close to rod A drawing warp in to weaving width of belt. You are now ready to weave. (See photo H24.)

Winding the Shuttle

Step 1—Take the small dowel with pointed ends. Lay a length of weft yarn along dowel and wind yarn around it to hold.

Step 2—Spiral yarn around dowel to end where taper begins.

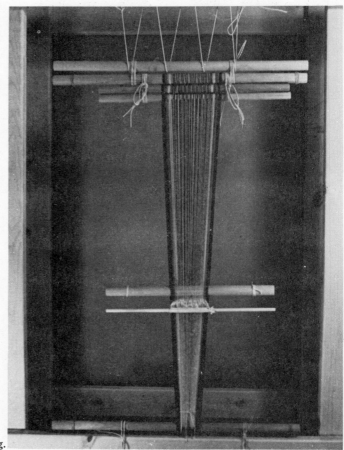

Photo H24. Hopi loom ready for weaving.

Photo H25. Hopi shuttle partially wound with two-ply cotton.

Step 3—Wind around once or twice at this point.

Step 4—Spiral yarn around dowel to other end where taper begins. Wind around once or twice.

Step 5—Spiral yarn to other end and wind around tapered end, working closer to point each time.

Step 6—Continue as established until you have a quantity of yarn on shuttle and tapered points are completely covered. (See photo H25.)

Things to Know
Before You Start to Weave

- How to Make the Sheds
- How to Use your Batten/Beater and Shuttle
- Warp Tension
- How to Handle your Weft
- How to Splice Weft
- How to Advance Weaving
- Weaving Aids

How to Make the Sheds

The shed is the opening made when half the warps are brought forward. There are two sheds.

The *stick* shed, produced when all warps on front of this stick are forward, and the *pull* shed, produced when all warps in heddles are forward. Any other sheds necessary to do this weave are made by picking up warp threads with your fingers.

To make the stick shed grasp both the shed stick and the heddle stick with both hands at either side and move them down a few inches, up a few inches and down a few inches together. Once should do it. If you move them up and down more than is necessary, you are just wearing out and fuzzing up your warp. (See photo H26.) After this up/

Photo H26. Making the stick shed.

down movement is completed the sticks should be in the upper part of your warp away from the woven area. The warps will be separated by the thickness of your shed stick. When shed is open, insert your batten/beater in a vertical position through the shed, then turn it horizontally to hold shed open.

To make the pull shed move the shed stick to top of warp. With left hand pull forward and move heddle stick up and down so it is about halfway between woven web and shed stick. With end of your batten, strum warp above heddle stick to help separate the warp threads. Then move heddle stick up and down and strum again. (See photo H27.) When a clear shed is achieved, insert batten in shed, then turn horizontally to hold shed open.

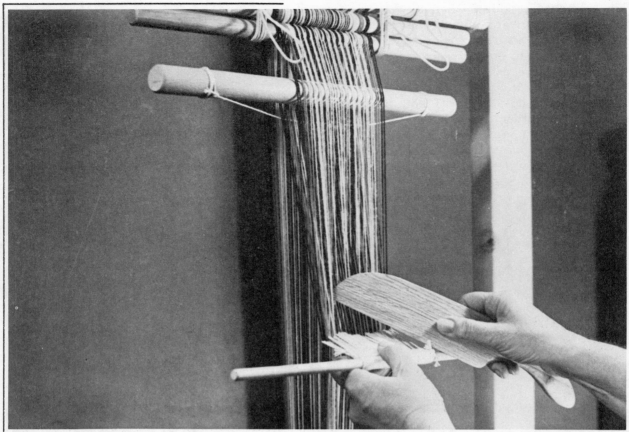

Photo H27. Strumming the warp with batten/beater to help clear the pull shed.

The stick shed is easy to make but the pull shed is always sticky. What usually happens is that some of the back warp threads stick and are drawn forward with the threads in the heddles. Here's a tip that will help you be sure you have the correct warps forward for the pull shed. After shed is made and batten has been inserted, move batten up to shed stick (while still in shed) and see if the threads cross correctly between shed stick and batten. If they don't, it will be easy to detect as the incorrect ones will float over both stick and batten.

How to Use Your Batten/Beater and Shuttle

Your batten/beater serves two purposes: It holds the shed open while you pass your shuttle and it serves as the beater to beat the weft into place.

Step 1—Open the shed. Insert the batten in a vertical position. With fine edge of batten down, beat preceding weft into place; that is, holding batten with both hands, push down hard on weft. This movement places the weft and straightens the warp at the web line. (See photo H28.)

Step 2—Raise batten and turn it horizontally to hold shed open.

Step 3—Pass the shuttle through this shed *below* batten. (See photo H29.)

Photo H28. Correct way to beat with batten. First two rows of weaving completed.

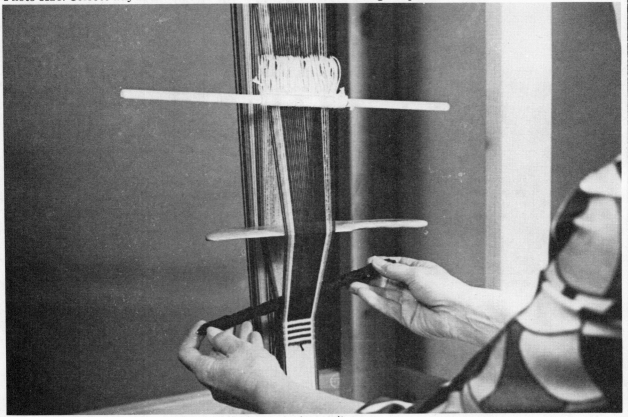

Photo H29. Putting shuttle through shed held open by batten/beater.

Step 4—Turn batten vertically and remove.

Step 5—Change to next shed and before you turn the batten horizontally, beat last weft into place.

The harder you beat the weft the tighter and heavier the fabric will be and the shorter the floats. I find it a good practice to gently push the weft down as you remove the batten then finish placing it when you beat on the next shed.

Be sure to put an even pressure on the batten or your weaving will build up higher on one side.

The above procedure will vary somewhat when you are doing the pick-up pattern areas and we will note the variation at that time.

Warp Tension

We have mentioned before that in winding the warp each thread should be pulled to the same tension. Weft lines will not lay straight if warp tension is uneven. The warp must be tight for the weaving but not as tight as for rug weaving described earlier. Too tight a warp makes it difficult to make the pick-up. Too loose a warp gives you poor edges and your batten and shed stick keep falling out. A little experimentation will help you decide on the right tension. Don't ignore an incorrect warp tension. Take time to get it right.

How to Handle Your Weft

You should use a cotton weft that has little or no elasticity. The important thing is that the weft lay flat at the edges. The tightness of the warp causes your weft to ripple and if not corrected a bad edge results. Handle your weft as follows:

Step 1—When shuttle has been passed through the shed, say right to left, on right side hook weft around middle finger and pull weft with left hand so it is taut. This straightens the weft out on the row below.

Step 2—While holding weft taut, with thumbnail and index finger of right hand over weft push warp threads to desired closeness.

Step 3—Hold as you draw weft to left through shed and off middle finger. (See photo H30.)

Step 4—Hold weft tension and remove batten.

Step 5—Change shed. Insert batten and beat weft into place.

How to Splice Weft Yarn

When you run out of weft, lay end of weft into next shed, overlap new weft with old weft for about 1″ and continue weaving in the same direction.

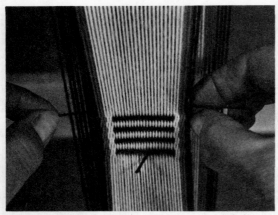

Photo H30. How to hold weft taut to keep edges straight.

How to Advance Weaving

When your weaving is too high for comfort and the shed is hard to pull open, you should lower the weaving area.

Step 1—Loosen the cord at top of loom and relax tension of warp.

Step 2—Insert batten in a shed and with hands on both ends of batten, push down weaving. Warp will move through loom rods at top of loom and the woven area will advance up the back of the loom.

Step 3—When you have weaving positioned where you wish, tighten tension again.

Weaving Aids

Some of you may have difficulty in seeing to do the pick-up. Dark against dark and light against light give little contrast. To aid you in seeing the pick-up, pin a contrasting colored paper behind the pick-up area. This paper can be pinned to the back layer of warp.

Take time to get comfortable. Fasten your loom and see how far your weaving area will be from the floor. Take time to find the right thing to sit on, something that is the correct height. You do not want to hold your arms too high all the time. The area you are weaving should be more or less directly in front of your face. If it is too low, you will have trouble seeing the correct threads. If it's too high, your arms and shoulders will ache. If you sit on the floor, grab a pillow.

Be sure you have good light. Pick-up weaves are exacting and you must be able to see every thread. A light coming over your right or left shoulder would be ideal. Do not face a window.

Take time to get comfortable. Weaving is fun. Being comfortable helps it to be that way.

Beginning the Weaving

We will begin our project with basic steps to make you familiar with the weave. Our first directions will be for weaving plain weave with no pick-up. We will achieve horizontal stripes in the center section.

Step 1—Open the stick shed.

Step 2—Insert batten and turn it horizontally to hold shed open.

Step 3—Put the shuttle through the shed from right to left and draw weft yarn through leaving about 2″ or so of yarn extended on the right side.

Step 4—Remove batten. Place weft about 8″ above the knots in warp at rod A. This unwoven area is for fringe.

Step 5—Change shed; that is, push shed stick to top of warp and pull heddle stick forward. The warp will be sticky so strum the warp with the end of your batten until the threads separate. (See How to Make the Pull Shed, page 121.)

Step 6—Insert batten and turn horizontally.

Step 7—Take end of the weft on right, turn it back into the shed and pull it to the front in middle of warp.

Step 8—Put the shuttle through the warp from left to right and pull weft through. A good place to lay your shuttle while hands are busy with other details is on top of rod A between front and back warp layers.

Step 9—Pull weft with right hand, drawing the warp threads together so they just touch. This will narrow your warp to under 2″. This is a warp face weave so the weft should not show through the warp in the plain weave areas and very little in pattern areas.

Step 10—Turn batten vertically and remove.

Step 11—Change to stick shed. Insert batten.

Step 12—Beat weft. (See How to Use Your Batten/Beater and Shuttle, page 122 and photo H28.)

Step 13—Raise batten and turn horizontally. Before you proceed, check to be sure you have drawn warp sufficiently close to cover weft. Now refer to How to Handle Your Weft (page 124) and continue this plain weave until you can manipulate the two sheds and can get a good edge. End with weft on right.

Floated Warp Pattern

Our next section of weaving will be to introduce a pick-up pattern. It is necessary that you thoroughly understand what you want to achieve. Let's discuss the weave construction.

This is a weave in which some warp threads *float* over the surface while the rest of the threads weave plain. By float we mean that the warp will lie on the front or back surface of the fabric and not always be caught into the weave by every weft.

Each warp thread that is picked or dropped will float over three wefts or float under three wefts depending on whether you refer to front or back warp. The only exception to this is that you may choose to float over five wefts at the reverse point of your design.

The one thing you want to keep in mind is that whenever you pick up a warp thread from the back warp you must drop a warp thread from the front warp. However, there is one exception to this rule. (See Eliminating the Dot, page 135.)

Let us discuss terminology. Whenever we say

pick we mean that you will reach through the front warp and pick up a warp thread from the back warp.

Whenever we say *drop* we mean that you will drop the next warp from the front warp. Warps that are picked and dropped are always adjacent to each other.

Whenever we say *transfer* we mean taking the next front warp from one hand and putting it in the other hand.

Whenever we say *weave* we mean for you to take the weft through the shed as established for whatever distance is specified.

Front warp means all warps brought forward when shed is made.

Back warp means all warps left in back when the shed is made.

Also keep in mind that the edge stripes, the first twelve warps on either side of your sample, are always woven plain weave (over one, under one, over, under, etc.) except as discussed under Eliminating the Dot.

Single Pick-up Pattern Row—Now let us do a single pick-up pattern row with brown pattern on front, cream pattern on back. Weft on right.

Step 1—Stick shed. Beat last weft into place. Put fingers of left hand into shed and remove batten.

Step 2—On right side, take the first six front warp threads into your right hand (edge stripes). Now slightly pull apart the groups in each hand. This exposes the first brown thread of the back warp of the center section.

Step 3—Pick up this first brown back warp thread with right hand. (See photo H31.)

Photo H31. Step 3, Floated Warp Pattern—Picking up (P) first brown back warp thread in center section.

127

Step 4—Drop the next front cream warp thread from your left hand. (See photo H32.)

Step 5—Transfer the next front warp thread from your left hand to your right hand. (See photo H33.) We will henceforth refer to these three steps

Photo H32. Step 4, Floated Warp Pattern—Dropping (D) first cream front warp thread in center section.

Photo H33. Step 5, Floated Warp Pattern—Transferring (T) second cream front warp thread from left to right hand.

as P for pick, D for drop, T for transfer, or PDT. *Across warp* will mean center section only.

Step 6—Continue to PDT across warp. You are picking the first, third, fifth, seventh and all odd-numbered back warp threads. End with pick, drop and six warps remaining in left hand.

Step 7—Transfer all warps in right hand to left hand. Insert batten in this new shed made with your fingers and turn horizontally. (See photo H34.)

Photo H34. Step 7, Floated Warp Pattern—Picked up shed ready to weave.

Step 8—Pass shuttle through this shed right to left. Adjust weft tension.

Step 9—Pull shed. Beat. You can now see that the picked-up warp threads are floating. Weave left to right.

Step 10—Stick shed. Weave right to left.

Step 11—Pull shed. Weave left to right. (See photo H35.)

Double Pick-up Pattern Row—Now let's do a double pick-up pattern row.

I will no longer mention the details of the actual weaving—inserting batten, beating, passing shuttle, adjusting weft tension, etc. I will assume that you know when to do these things.

Step 1—Repeat Steps 1 through 9 for single row pick-up preceding.

Step 2—Stick shed. Put left hand in shed and remove batten.

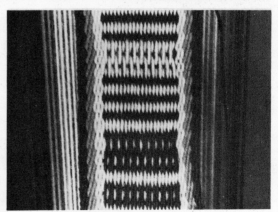

Photo H35. Bottom to top:
    Single pick-up pattern row
    Double pick-up pattern row
    Plain weave area
    Double pick-up pattern row,
      reverse color.

Step 3—On right side take first seven front warp threads in right hand. Slightly pull apart the two groups. This exposes the *second* thread of the back warp center section.

Step 4—Pick this second warp from back, drop one from front, transfer next front warp from left hand to right hand. PDT across warp. You are picking the second, fourth, sixth and all even-numbered back warp threads. In other words you are picking the back warp threads you didn't pick before. End with PD and seven front warps remaining in left hand.

Step 5—Transfer warps in right hand to left hand. Weave right to left.

Step 6—Pull shed. Insert batten and beat. (See photo H35.) Weave left to right.

Step 7—Stick shed. Weave a few more rows of plain weave as we have done or you can do the first row of pick-up again to get a larger pattern area. I'm sure you see by now that you alternate the pick-up rows. You are first picking up the odd-numbered and then the even-numbered back warps. You pick up on the stick shed going right to left and do plain weave on the pull shed left to right. This gives you a dark pattern on front, cream pattern on back.

Practice these two pick-up rows until you have them down pat.

Reverse Coloring—To reverse the coloring and have cream pattern on front and brown on the back, proceed as follows:

Row 1—Stick shed. Weft on right. Weave plain right to left.

Row 2—Pull shed. Take front warp in right hand, transfer first six front warps on left to left hand. This exposes the first cream back warp of center section. Pick this warp with left hand, drop next front brown warp from right hand. Transfer next front brown warp from right hand to left hand. Proceed PDT across warp.

Row 3—Stick shed. Plain weave right to left.

Row 4—Pick up on this row beginning with *second* center section back warp thread and proceed PDT across warp. The same rules apply except you are picking up on the pull shed going left to right and weaving plain on the stick shed right to left. (See photo H35.) Do a few rows of plain weave ending on the right side.

Floated Warp Pattern with Plain Background

In this section of weaving we will add a picked-up pattern on a plain weave background. We will pick going right to left on stick shed and weave plain left to right on pull shed.

Row 1—Stick shed. Left hand in shed. Transfer sixteen front warps to right hand. Pick one brown, drop one cream. Transfer all to left hand. Insert batten but be careful to retain picked and dropped thread positions. Weave right to left.

Row 2—Pull shed. Weave left to right. The center brown warp thread floats. (See photo H36.)

Photo H36. Row 2, Floated Warp Pattern with Plain Background—One warp picked from back and one warp dropped from front to begin picked up design.

Row 3—Stick shed. Take front warps in left hand. Transfer fifteen warps to right hand. PDT, PD. You have picked the two brown on either side of the center floating warp. Weave right to left.

From here on we will give you only information for the stick shed weaving right to left. The pull shed will always be plain weave left to right.

Row 5—Stick shed. T 14 front warps to right hand. PDT 2 times, PD. (three floating warps)

Row 7—Stick shed. T 13 to right hand. PD, T 5, PD.

Row 9—Stick shed. T 12 to right hand. PDT, PD, T 3, PDT, PD. (two pair of floating warps separated by three cream warps)

Row 11—Stick shed. T 11 to right hand. PD, T 9, PD. (two floating warps separated by nine cream warps)

Row 13—Stick shed. T 10, PDT, PD, T 7, PDT, PD.

Row 15—Stick shed. T 9, PD, T 13, PD.

Row 17—Stick shed. T 8, PDT, PD, T 11, PDT, PD.

Row 19—Stick shed. T 7, PD, T 17, PD.

Row 21—Stick shed. T 6, PDT, PD, T 15, PDT, PD.

Continue and finish design in your own fashion. Keep in mind when you pick one, you must drop one and on one row you are picking even numbers and the next row odd numbers. You do not pick same warp thread in two rows straight.

Check to see if back is an exact reverse of the front.

You will notice that your weaving measures less than the first area of plain weave. Whenever you do pattern and have warp floats, the weaving narrows. At this point your warp should measure about 1¾″ wide. Your warp will narrow even more when weaving the next section. (See photo H42.)

Be sure you understand the preceding thoroughly before continuing.

Your weaving is probably by now so high that you have to reach up and there is less space between the woven area and the shed rods above. It is time to advance the weaving. (See How to Advance Weaving, page 125.)

Sticky Heddles

I'm sure you have noticed that the fibers from the wool warp are balling up on the heddles and getting sticky. If you did not respin your warp tight enough, it will fuzz on the heddles even more.

Take time to pick this wool from the heddles. If it gets too bad, it will cause you to miss threads when making your sheds. (See photo H37.)

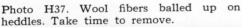
Photo H37. Wool fibers balled up on heddles. Take time to remove.

Floated Warp in Reverse Color

Here's the weave the experienced Hopi weavers do. You know from previous weaving (See Single and Double Pick-Up Pattern Rows, pages 127 and 129) that it takes two rows to complete a pick-up area. You pick up going one direction and you weave plain coming back. We will now have pick-up areas and plain weave areas on each row. What is a plain weave area on one row, will be a pick-up area on the next row and vice versa.

We will do a simple diamond for our design. On the first row going right to left in the stick shed, we will pick up the right background, weave plain over center diamond area, then pick up left background area. On the second row in pull shed going left to right, we will weave plain the left background area, pick up the center diamond area and weave plain right background area. That will be the sequence of each two rows.

For clarification of copy we will add these additional abbreviations: *Begin pick-up with first back warp in center section* will be written BEG 1ST. *Begin pick-up with second back warp in center section* will be written BEG 2ND. *Number of times* will be written X and as before P for pick, D for drop, T for transfer.

Before beginning on the next sample, let us discuss short rows.

Short Rows

If you have done any weaving at all, you know that the take-up of the warp is different in plain weave areas and pattern weave areas. When the warp thread goes under and over every weft, it takes up more than when it goes under three wefts and over three wefts as in this technique.

The twelve edge threads on either side are woven plain all the time and so they take up more than the center section which is woven in pattern most of the way for our next sample. If you were to continue to weave your belt without allowing for this take-up variation, you would soon find the edge threads getting tighter than the center. The final result would be a rippled effect with the center bulging out and not laying flat.

To take care of this take-up variation in the warp we weave *short rows*. That is, we weave the center without weaving the edge threads. A good place to do these short rows is where a design reverses or in between design changes.

If you will remember to do this a number of times throughout your project, the tension of your edge threads and center section will stay even. The next section will incorporate short rows in the weaving.

Photo H38. Row 5, Floated Warp in Reverse Color—Backgrounds picked and dropped and three transferred for center diamond.

Photo H39. Row 6, Floated Warp in Reverse Color—Two warps picked on either side of diamond point.

Photo H40. Row 19—First short row.

Begin with weft on right, stick shed. All odd-numbered rows will be the stick shed and all even-numbered rows will be the pull shed. We will not list each shed.

Row 1—BEG 1ST. PDT across. (All background)

Row 2—Plain weave. You have completed a single pick-up pattern row.

Row 3—BEG 2ND. PDT across.

Row 4—T 16 to left hand. (This left background to weave plain.) P 1, D 1. (Diamond area picked up) T remaining warps to left hand. (Right background area to weave plain) *Note:* The warp you picked up must be on front of weft in row below and the warp you dropped must be on back of weft in row below.

Row 5—BEG 1ST. PDT 4x, PD. (Right background picked up) T 3 (Diamond to weave plain) PDT 4x, PD. (Left background picked up) (See photo H38.)

Row 6—T 15, PDT, PD, T 15. (See photo H39.)

Row 7—BEG 2ND. PDT 3x, PD, T 5, PDT 4x.

Row 8—T 14, PDT 2x, PD, T 14.

Continue as established transferring one less each time in background on pull shed and transferring two more each time in diamond area on stick shed until you are to row 18 which will be:

Row 18—T 9, PDT 7x, PD, T 9.

Reversing with plain weave short rows.

Row 19—Stick shed. Drop six left edge threads off batten and weave plain. First short row. (See photo H40.)

Row 20—Pull shed. Drop six right and left edge threads off batten and weave plain. Second short row. (See photo H41.)

Row 21—Stick shed. Drop six right edge threads and weave plain. Third short row. You are weaving only the center section.

Row 22—Begin reverse design. T 9, PDT 7x, PD, T 9.

Row 23—BEG 1ST. PDT, PD, T 15, PDT, PD.

Row 24—T 10, PDT 6x, PD, T 10.

Row 25—BEG 2ND. PDT, PD, T 13, PDT 2x.

Row 26—T 11, PDT 5x, PD, T 11.

Row 27—BEG 1ST. PDT 2x, PD, T 11, PDT 2x, PD.

Row 28—T 12, PDT 4x, PD, T 12.

Continue as established transferring one more on background on pull shed and transferring two less in diamond on each stick shed. When you get to row 37 it will be:

Row 37—BEG 2ND. PDT 4x, PD, T 1, PDT 5x.

Row 38—Weave plain.

Row 39—BEG 1ST. PDT across warp.

Row 40—Weave plain. (See top design of photo H42.)

Your weaving has narrowed again and should measure about 1⅝″ wide. You can now see why it is difficult to combine plain weave areas and pattern weave areas in one project.

Eliminating the Dot

I think I should explain now about one of the finer points of this weave before you discover the dot and wonder.

If you will look on the reverse side of your belt you will find a row of dark dots on the reverse of the right side. They happen every other row. (See photo H47, about midway on reverse side at dark diamond.) There is a way to correct this.

On the pattern rows that begin BEG 2ND you can drop the fourth cream warp of the outside stripe area on the right before you begin the pick-up. This will make the cream warp float on the back side and cover this dot. It also makes your stripe a little narrower.

If you had wound your warp so that you had five cream warps on the right instead of the left, you would end up with a dark dot on the left front side. To cover it, you would have to pick up a cream warp of the left stripe. Either way you do it, you are borrowing from the stripe to cover the dot.

My directions do not tell you to drop this cream warp as mentioned above. I didn't want to complicate the directions. You can, of course, do this if you wish.

Reversing Your Pattern Design

There are two ways to reverse the design when you are weaving floated warp in reverse color. One way is to weave three plain weave rows at the point of reversing as you have just done. The second way is to float the pattern warps over five wefts instead of three.

It is necessary to set up the proper sequence of pick-up before starting the reverse pattern. If you do not, there will be a flat area next to one side of your design because the background floats do not lay close enough to the pattern area. (See photo H43 showing incorrect reversing procedure and diagram H2 showing details of the weave.)

The next sample diamond design will reverse by floating pattern warps over five wefts.

Up until now we have been giving you directions including the transferring of the edge stripe warp threads. You should now have done enough weaving that you understand that these threads weave plain weave all the time. From here on we will give you the count referring to the center section only; that is, instead of saying T 16, PD, T 16,

Photo H41. Row 20—Second short row.

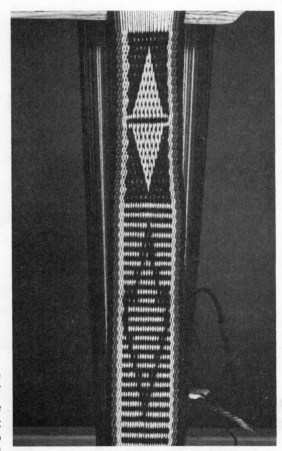

Photo H42. Bottom—Floated warp pattern with plain background.
Top—Floated warp pattern in reverse color.
Note variation in width.

we will say T 10, PD, T 10. You will automatically transfer the six edge warp threads on each shed.

Diamond design in floated warp in reverse color technique reversing with pattern warps floating over five wefts:

Row 1—Stick shed. Plain weave.

Row 2—Pull shed. T 10, PD, T 10. Continue as established for ten rows and you have five pattern floats and weft is on right side.

Row 11—Stick shed. BEG 1ST. PDT 2X, PD, T 11, PDT 2X, PD.

Row 12—T 6, PDT 4X, PD. (You pick the same warp threads as before.) T6.

Row 13—BEG 2ND. PDT 3X, PD, T 9, PDT 3X.

Row 14—T 7, PDT 3X, PD, T 7.

Row 15—BEG 1ST. PDT 3X, PD, T 7, PDT 3X, PD. Continue decreasing your diamond along lines established. (See photo H44 and diagram H2.)

Directions for a design with two pattern areas and three background areas: (See photo H45.)

Begin with weft on right. The count given is center section only. Outside stripes weave plain.

Row 1—BEG 2ND. PDT 2X, PD, T 9, PDT 2X, PD.

Row 2—T 7, PDT, PD, T 1, PDT, PD, T 7.

Row 3—BEG 1ST. PDT 3X, PD, T 3, PD, T 3, PDT 3X, PD.

Row 4—T 8, PD, T 3, PD, T 8.

Row 5—BEG 2ND. PDT, PD, T 5, PDT, PD, T 5, PDT, PD.

Row 6—T 5, PDT, PD, T 5, PDT, PD, T 5.

Row 7—BEG 1ST. PDT 2X, PD, T 3, PDT 2X, PD, T 3, PDT 2X, PD.

Row 8—T 6, PD, T 7, PD, T 6.

Row 9—BEG 2ND. PD, T 5, PDT 3X, PD, T 5, PDT.

Row 10—T 3, PDT, PD, T 9, PDT, PD, T 3.

Row 11—BEG 1ST. PDT, PD, T 3, PDT 4X, PD, T 3, PDT, PD.

Row 12—T 4, PD, T 11, PD, T 4.

Row 13—T 5, PDT 5X, PD, T 5.

Row 14—T 1, PDT, PD, T 13, PDT, PD, T 1.

Row 15—BEG 1ST. PD, T 3, PDT 6X, PD, T 3, PD.

Row 16—T 2, PD, T 15, PD, T 2.

Row 17—BEG 2ND. PDT across warp. (Weave short row.)

Row 18 is like Row 16. (Weave short row.) Continue in reverse Rows 15, 14, 13, 12, etc.

You have the method now of doing whatever design you wish. Finish weaving your belt. When the woven area reaches the top loom rods in the back and you have woven the front to within 10" of the top loom rods, your weaving is finished.

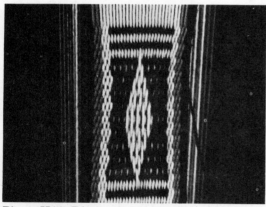

Photo H43. Diamond design reversed incorrectly. Pattern and background floats are separated on top half of diamond.

Photo H44. Diamond design reversed with pattern warps floating over five wefts.

Photo H45. Design incorporating two pattern areas.

Review

Now that you have completed the various techniques on this setup, you can see that the Floated Warp in Reverse Color is the most difficult. Let us review and discuss some of the rules to remember.

Things that you should have observed: Except for sometimes on the left edge next to the stripe, you never end a pick-up area with PDT. You end with PD. That is, you would never PDT, PDT, T 9, etc. If you did, you would actually be transferring ten. It should be PDT, PD, T 9, etc.

On the stick shed rows, you alternate beginning the pick-up with the first back warp and the second back warp.

At the point of reversing a design, you must have the proper pick-up sequence. To clarify this refer to diagram H2a, b, c, and photograph H43. To keep the diagram less complicated, I have shown only the front surface warp threads in the detail. The dots represent the warps you transfer for the center pattern on the stick shed and for the back-

Diagram **H2**. Only the front surface warp threads are shown. The dots represent the warps you transfer for the center pattern on the stick shed and for the background on the pull shed. The vertical lines represent the warps you pick up for the center pattern on the pull shed and for the background on the stick shed. The dot and vertical line is a single float (each goes over one weft). Dot, line, dot together makes a three thread float.

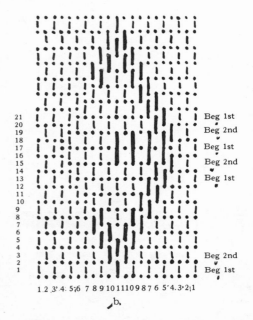

b—Alternate method of reversing design. Warps float over five wefts at widest point.

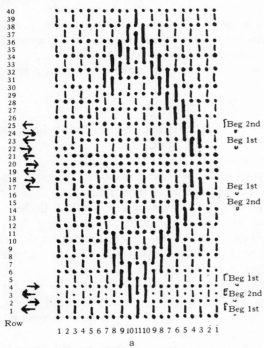

a—Correct way front surface is woven using plain weave where pattern reverses. Note how the background floats lay close to the pattern floats.

c—Incorrect way to reverse pattern. You must add two extra rows to keep the proper sequence of picked up threads. If you do not add these rows, on one end of the diamond the floats of the background and the pattern will be separated by a line of single floats, as show in this diagram and in photo H43.

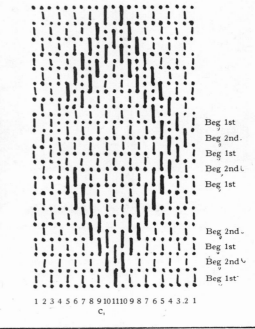

ground on the pull shed. The vertical lines represent the warps you pick up for the center pattern on the pull shed and for the background on the stick shed. We will refer to the dot and the vertical line as a single float; that is, each goes over one weft. When you put a dot, line, dot together, you have a three-thread float.

Diagram a shows correct way the front surface is woven using plain weave where pattern reverses. Note how the background floats lay close to the pattern floats.

Diagram b shows the alternate method for reversing design. Warps float over five wefts at widest point.

Diagram c and photo H43 show the incorrect way to reverse pattern. You must add two extra rows to keep the proper sequence of picked-up threads. If you do not add these rows, on one end of the diamond the floats of the background and the pattern will be separated by a line of single floats.

Whenever you pick one, you must drop one. It's a very simple rule with the only exception being at the edge of pattern area to cover the dot.

The edge stripes are always woven in plain weave. Only the center warp threads are floated. The same exception applies here, too.

Weave short rows at intervals to keep tension even.

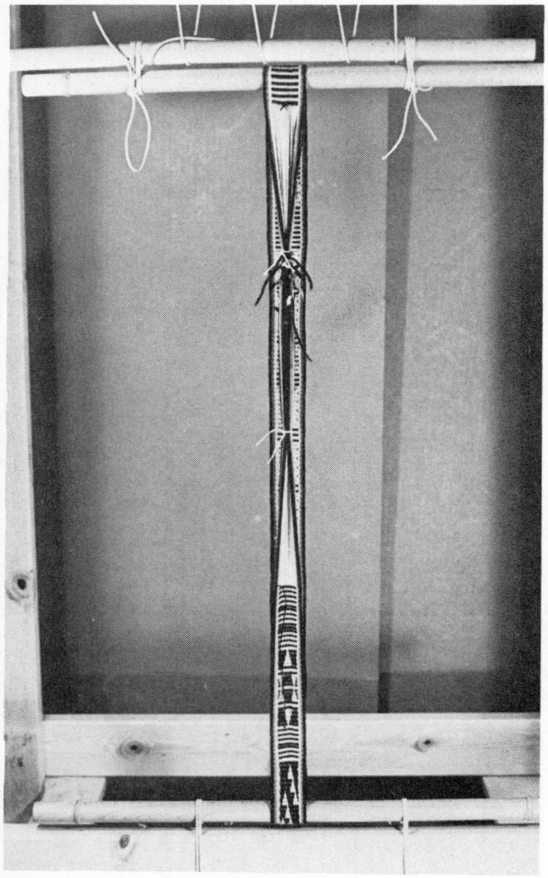

Removing Belt from Loom

Step 1—Fasten weft end by tying to outside warp with overhand knot.

Step 2—Remove heddle string.

Step 3—Untie and remove the two small loom rods tied to rod B at top of warp.

Step 4—Tighten tension of warp a little.

Step 5—Even up warp so weaving line is level. You can do this by inserting batten in stick shed and pushing down. At the same time, advance warp so knotted area is in front of you.

Step 6—Remove shed stick.

Step 7—Tie a string tightly around warp at knotted area. Do not have any knots between tie and beginning of weaving.

Step 8—Make another tie around warp the same distance from end of weaving as first tie is from beginning of weaving. (See photo H46.)

Step 9—Remove rod B at top of warp and rod A at bottom of warp and slip belt off rods.

Finishing Hopi Belt

Step 1—Cut warp above first tie. My Hopi instructor lays the belt on a hard surface and uses a sharp knife to cut the warp.

Step 2—Sprinkle cut ends with water to help

Photo H46. Removing belt from loom. Heddle, shed stick and small loom rods removed. Warp tied.

set the twist.

Step 3—Take each warp and respin it by laying warp thread on thigh and rolling it *away* from you with palm of hand or underside of thumb. Hold each one so it does not come unspun until you have four or five ends respun. Our sample will have five in each group. The tighter you respin the yarn the nicer your fringe will be.

Step 4—Take the fifth strand and knot it around the ends of the first four strands using an overhand knot.

Step 5—Even up all warp threads by pulling on ends. If you don't pull them good and straight, you will have bubbles in your fringe.

Step 6—Pull out straight and twist all five strands together by laying them on thigh and rolling them *toward* you with palm of hand.

Step 7—Repeat above for all warps. The last group will have six ends in it. Trim ends to make them even if you wish.

Step 8—Repeat above for other end of belt.

Step 9—Time to admire your finished product. (See photo H47.)

The narrow belts particularly have a tendency to spiral. Steam pressing will take care of this though it is un-Hopi.

Photo H47. Finished Hopi type belt.

When Problems Develop

If your edges are uneven, you are not handling your weft correctly, or your warp is too loose. Refer to Warp Tension and How to Handle Your Weft (page 124).

If your belt is wider in some areas than others, you did not pull the same tension on each weft. Your sample belt will be different width because you have plain weave areas and pattern areas and each weave draws in differently.

If pattern is distorted, you are not beating evenly. Be sure you are applying the same amount of pressure on the batten/beater each time and that you are getting the same number of picks (wefts) per inch.

If you have warp floats where they don't belong, you are not getting a true shed. There may be so much fuzz in the heddles that the warps will not separate properly. Or after you have made your pick up and your fingers are holding the newly created shed open, you may not be getting your batten in the same space as your fingers.

If you have weft floats on back, you are not getting your batten in the shed correctly. The end of batten is picking up warp threads from the back of the shed.

If you break a warp thread, fasten a new length at the knotted area and remove the broken one. Carry the new thread through the top loom rod area and heddle area like the broken one was and pin the end to your weaving at the correct tension. Be sure it is respun the same as original warp thread. When belt is off loom, thread ends in a tapestry needle and overlap in the weave 1″ to 2″. Since this is a warp face weave it is impossible to completely hide a warp splice.

If weaving is building up more on one side than the other, you are putting more pressure on one side than the other with your batten/beater or you may have wound a part of your warp tighter than the other part.

If your fringe does not hold a tight twist, you did not respin the individual warp threads tightly enough before you twisted the group together.

Analyzing Your Belt

The edges should be even and straight. You should have the same number of picks per inch throughout the belt. If not, your warp floats will not be the same length and your patterns will be distorted.

The center section should not bulge or ripple. Your weft should not show in plain weave areas and only very little in pattern areas.

The Embroidery Weave—Sash

The embroidery weave is a handsome weave used for the Hopi ceremonial sashes. The sashes are worn by the dancers in a kilt fashion. The ceremonial sash is made up of two identical pieces fastened together. There is a looped fringe at one end of each piece.

Let us analyze the weave of the sash. The name embroidery weave probably comes from the fact that it looks like embroidery. The wool yarn is not woven in but wrapped around warp threads causing the warp to stand out like ribs on the surface of the fabric. The fine cotton is woven in plain weave in back or in front of the wool yarn depending on the pattern arrangement. If you were to remove all the wool pattern yarn, you would still have a plain weave cloth though loosely woven. See diagram H3 for a cross-section view of this weave.

Diagram H3a. Plain embroidery weave

H3b. Pattern embroidery weave (MERVIN WOLFF)

The Navajo rug weave we discussed elsewhere in this book and the Hopi blanket weave is a weft face; that is, only the weft yarn shows. The warp is completely covered. The Hopi belt weave is a warp face weave as the weft is covered and only the warp shows. In this embroidery weave both warp and weft show in the plain weave areas.

In the early days the sash was woven by leaving a short area of warp unwoven for fringe at the beginning. Then a small white plain area was woven followed by the pattern area. The large area of white plain weave was woven last, so that one had to weave right up to the top twining as in the rug and blanket weaving. This meant that the last few inches were tedious and time-consuming to weave. In later years some of the weavers adopted another order for the weaving of the sashes. They now weave the large white area first, then the pattern area and end with the small white plain weave area thus leaving the unwoven area for the fringe at the top and eliminating the tedious last few inches of weaving. However, our sample will be woven the way they wove their sashes in the early years so you will know how to handle it. You can, of course, reverse the order if you wish.

Materials Needed

For loom rods—Three ¾" dowels, 18" to 24" long.

For stick shed—One ⅜" dowel, at least 12" long.

For heddle sheds—Two ¾₆″ or ¼″ dowels, at least 12″ long.

The Hopi, of course, in early times used branches or some such native material that was available.

Batten—1″ to 1½″ wide, about 16″ long and not too thin.

Comb (fork)

Pointed stick about 10″ to 12″ long

2 shuttles—¼″ dowels with both ends pointed

Heavy cord for tying loom rods

Cord for heddles, 8/4 cotton carpet warp will do

Cord for binding and twining, 8-ply cotton will do

Toothpick

For stretcher—wood about 10″ long, ¾″ wide, ⅛″ to ¾₆″ thick.

2 small finishing nails or equivalent.

Most of these materials are the same as used for the Hopi belt or Navajo rug.

Yarn

Warp

Warp—8/4 cotton warp or equivalent in white or natural. Sometimes the Hopi use a heavier cotton.

Weft

Weft—For tabby or plain weaving in the pattern areas, fine white cotton. Use number 8 sewing thread or 24/3 or a little heavier weaving cotton. For white sections, a heavy cotton, eight-ply or equivalent thickness. I've seen a few sashes with this area woven with wool. For pattern, four-ply knitting worsted. Black, green and red would be typical Hopi colors and sometimes a bright royal blue.

Twining cord—This is often the same size and color as the selvage cord or it can be white.

Selvage cord—Two- or three-ply wool yarn. Not too heavy. Usually in a color.

The Hopi weavers in the early days handspun their yarns but they have been using commercial yarns for quite a long time.

Amount of Yarn Required

Each piece of a typical Hopi sash would measure about 40″ long plus fringe and anywhere from 9″ to 12″ wide. You need two identical pieces.

Our sample sash will be smaller. It will be 8″ x 25″ including fringe. The warp should be set twenty to twenty-two ends per inch.

Warp needed—about 240 yards for the two pieces

Heavy cotton—about 70 yards

Four-ply knitting worsted and fine cotton—about 50 yards of each

Twining cord—about 3 yards

Selvage cord—about 4 yards

The amounts are figured for weaving ten picks per inch in the heavy cotton areas and sixteen picks per inch of each yarn in the pattern areas. A *pick* is a weft after it is woven.

For selvage you will need four pieces each about twice the length of your warp plus 24″.

Winding the Warp

You may use either type of warping frame, the one shown in the Navajo rug weaving section or the one used for the Hopi belt weave. Assemble frame as instructed.

Generally follow the instructions given in Winding the Warp (page 32). For this warp you will be winding more ends per inch. You do not need to mark off the dowel. As you wind, place the warp loops close on the dowel rods in groups of five loops (ten ends). For the sample wind seventeen groups, a total of 170 warp ends. End on same dowel as you began. When finished, push loops close together but do not let them cross over or get on top of each other. (See photo H48.)

Photo H48. Warp is placed on warping frame rod in groups of five loops. This makes it easy to count.

Twining to Space the Warp

Follow instructions as given in Twining to Space the Warp (page 33) but with the following changes: The twining cord should be 48" doubled to measure 24". On the loop end, tie a knot 6" in from end and cut loop.

With knot you can untie later, tie these 6" ends on dowel about 5" to left of warp. Have original knot and long ends hanging in front. Read the directions but make the following changes: Take one end of the twining cord under first warp loop left to right and as you pull twining cord you draw warp over to twining cord knot. Take this strand to left over other strand and pick up other strand from underneath. This is a little different from the twining given for Navajo rug weaving. Please compare photographs N17 and H49. As you twine,

Photo H49. Twining to space warps. This is different than the twining for rug set up. Compare this photo with N17.

you are moving your warp to the left. With your left thumb hold each twist between warps to keep cord tension tight. You want the warp loops as close together as you can get them.

To Establish Good Working Habits

Your left hand has to hold the twining cord tight so your right hand can find the right warp, pass the cord underneath and pull it down moving warp loop to left hand area. To do this efficiently, hold twining cord between thumb and index finger of right hand. Put middle finger of right hand under the correct warp right to left. Release cord held with thumb and index finger and slip index finger under warp with middle finger. Take cord between these two fingers and draw through to right and down to left hand area. (See photo H50.)

When you reach the last warp loop, knot ends of twining cord with knot close to warp.

To twine other end, you tie your twining cord about 5″ to the right of the warp and twine right to left drawing warp to right. The twining on this end is done as shown for Navajo rug weaving except you are beginning on right side instead of left.

When both ends are twined they should measure about 8″ on rods.

Securing the Cross

Same as explained previously, see page 34.

Removing Warp from Frame and Binding Warp to Loom Rods

Place loom rod next to warping frame dowel rod and tie ends of twining cord to loom rod. Repeat on other end of warp. (See photo H51.)

Loosen frame rods and remove from warp. The warp is now fastened only to the loom rods by ends of twining cords.

Now follow directions given for Binding Warp to Loom Rods (page 35), with the following changes: Instead of binding between every loop

Photo H50. Efficient way to handle twining cord: Left hand keeps tension, right hand takes cord under warp end.

Photo H51. Tie twining cord to loom rod before removing from warping frame. Repeat on other end.

Photo H52. First heddle stick is prepared and pushed to bottom of warp. Shed stick is at top. Use pointed stick to help count off warps and pick up every fifth pair in preparation for making pattern heddle stick. Insert another stick to hold picked up pairs as you work across warp.

Photo H53. Preparing pattern heddle stick located between other heddle and shed sticks.

or every pair of loops, bind between every four or five warp loops.

Mounting Warp in Loom Frame

Follow directions as explained on page 38.

Tensioning of Warp

Follow directions on page 40, but for this warp we want a medium tension, not as tight as for rug weaving.

Inserting Shed Sticks into Warp

Same as explained on page 40.

Making Heddles

Follow directions as given on page 41 except that you should make the heddles like the ones shown for Hopi belt weaving. (Refer to photos H17 and H18.) Use the $\frac{3}{16}''$ or $\frac{1}{4}''$ size dowel for heddle stick. When you have made a heddle around every other warp thread, push the heddle stick to bottom of warp. You now need another heddle stick to control the pattern threads.

With your batten still in shed and in vertical position, begin on left. Using pointed stick as a tool, count over four warp threads (two on top of batten and two on back), pick up with fingers of left hand the next two warp threads (one from top, one from back), count over eight warps (four on top and four on back) and pick up next two warps. Continue across picking up every ninth and tenth warp. You will have four left on the right side.

If you can't hold all the picked-up warps in your hand as you work right, slip in the other heddle stick temporarily to hold place. (See photo H52.)

Remove batten from where it is and insert it in this new shed.

You will now make heddles around the pairs of warps on front of the batten. (See photo H53.)

Selvage Threads

Read about The Navajo Selvage (page 48), to familiarize yourself with the various ways to handle the selvage. One Hopi weaver handles his selvage differently again. The right selvage thread is taken under the bottom loom rod, the two strands twisted clockwise (to the right), taken in back of the heddle sticks and in front of the shed stick and tied to the upper loom rod. The left selvage is looped on bottom loom rod, twisted clockwise, taken in back of the shed stick and heddle sticks and tied to upper loom rod. Every time he inserts his batten in the stick shed, the right selvage is always in front and the left selvage in back of the batten. If you handle your selvage this way, when you make the pattern shed, you always begin by putting batten tip behind right selvage before going through the shed.

As the Hopi weaver splits and twists the selvage during the weaving, he is taking out the twist he put in. The right selvage weaves by itself and the left selvage weaves with the outside warp thread. Why this weaver prefers to weave them differently from each other, I do not know. I've seen them weave with both right and left selvage threads held in front of the batten. It seems to be a matter of personal choice.

In sash weaving you split and twist each selvage *every other row* in the plain weave areas. On one row you split and twist the right selvage and on the next row you split and twist the left selvage. You always split and twist the selvage opposite the bound end of the weft; that is, you are always weaving *out* through the split selvage.

When you get to the pattern weaving, you treat the selvage the same for each two rows of weaving; that is, what you do to the selvage on the pattern row, you do on the tabby row that follows.

Securing the Shed Stick

Tie a heavy string around the right end of the shed stick, take it behind the right selvage threads, behind the warp, in front of the left selvage threads and tie to left side of shed stick. Leave a little slack in it. This prevents your shed stick from falling out and losing the cross. (See photo H54.)

Now you can remove the string that secured the cross and you are ready to weave.

Winding the Shuttle

Refer to that section under Hopi belt weaving (page 119).

The pattern yarn is not put on a shuttle. Prepare it this way: Wrap the four-ply wool between your little finger and thumb in a figure eight movement for twenty-five or so times. Remove from fingers and wrap around and around the middle a number of times until you have a long thin bundle. Tie end. Now you will use the end that you began with and draw yarn from the inside. We call this a butterfly. (See photo H55.)

How to Make the Stick and Pull Sheds

Please refer to page 43.

Beginning the Weaving

We will be leaving warp unwoven for fringe at the bottom so begin as follows:

Row 1—Stick shed. Insert a piece of wood or heavy cardboard about 1″ wide in the shed.

Row 2—Pull shed. Insert another piece of wood or cardboard in this shed. This leaves the

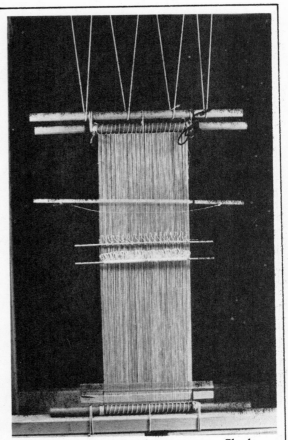

Photo H54. Loom ready to weave. Shed stick secured with string and selvage threads added. Two sticks have been woven in at bottom.

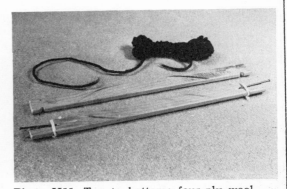

Photo H55. Top to bottom: four-ply wool yarn wound into a "butterfly." Stretcher with notches and channels carved out. Stretcher with string added and nails in place under string and in channels.

warp unwoven for a fringe. If you want a longer fringe, add more wood pieces or make them wider. (See photo H54.)

Row 3—Stick shed. Insert batten. For beginning only, to fasten weft yarn, split selvage on both sides by opening the two strands from the bottom loom rod. All twists are above batten on both sides. Take heavy cotton and lay about 1″ into the right edge through selvage threads. Bring both selvage threads on right to front of batten, then weave right to left. You are weaving out through the split selvage on the left. Grasp batten on both sides and beat hard. Remove batten.

Row 4—Pull shed. Insert batten and beat. Split and twist selvage on right by putting one strand on back of batten, using the strand that the weft did not weave around on row below. Be sure you are untwisting the twists you put in. Weave. Beat with batten and remove.

Row 5—Stick shed. Insert batten and beat with batten. Split and twist selvage on left by bringing one strand forward to front of batten. Be sure you are untwisting the twists above. Weave, beat with batten and remove.

Continue until you have several inches woven with white cotton. On the stick shed you are splitting and twisting the left selvage and on the pull shed you are splitting and twisting the right selvage. Every weft weaves out through the split selvage.

Use the comb to supplement the beating if you cannot get it tight enough with the batten. Fasten off your heavy white yarn by laying about 1″ back into the pull shed on the right.

Using the Stretcher

In the pattern area this embroidery weave draws in a great deal and so a stretcher is used to help keep the fabric to desired width.

Take a piece of wood about 10″ long and ⅛″ or so thick and about ¾″ wide. Carve notches on each side about 8″ apart, the width you wish to keep your fabric. Carve out a small channel just below these notches in the middle of the width. Tie a string around at the notched area. (See photo H55.)

Use two small finishing nails to fasten fabric to stretcher. The nails go through the edge of the fabric under the string and the point of the nail follows the channel as you push it through.

Fasten this stretcher about ½″ below weaving line. (See photo H56.) As you weave, keep moving this stretcher up.

Splicing Weft Yarns

The fine white cotton weft and heavy cotton weft are spliced by overlapping about 1″ in the shed

and continuing weaving in the same direction. However, the wool pattern weft is another problem.

This wool yarn is never held in place by the warp. It is either laying on front or back of the fabric. After your pattern weaving is started, you can end and begin a wool weft by pushing the end down into a pocket formed by the previous pattern weaving. The Hopi weaver uses a toothpick to do this. (See photo H59.)

Embroidery Weaving

We will give you directions for several design ideas you can try to get you acquainted with the weave and its possibilities.

Plain Embroidery Weave

Row 1—Pattern shed. Pick up right selvage as you insert batten. Split selvage on left. Take four-ply wool yarn wound in butterfly manner and push end to back between selvage thread and warp on right side. Take yarn behind selvage and over first four warps and under the first pair on front of batten. With left hand pick up the first two pairs of warps on front of batten and with right hand pass wool yarn in back. In so doing you are wrapping yarn around first pair. Pull yarn down toward weaving line. Pick up second and third pairs and pass yarn in back. You have now wrapped yarn

Photo H56. First area of heavy white is woven. Stretcher has been fastened to cloth to keep fabric to desired width. First row of pattern and first row of fine white cotton has been woven.

149

around the second pair of warps. Continue across warp and take yarn out through split selvage. The wool yarn is wrapped around every pair of warps on front of batten, and in between it covers the other warp threads. Remove batten.

Row 2—Stick shed. Insert batten and beat. Split selvage on left the same as pattern row below. Pass fine cotton through shed leaving 1″ on right side. Turn this 1″ of fine cotton around one strand of selvage and lay in shed. Beat with batten and remove. Beat with comb. With pointed stick push weft down even more, particularly around the wrap areas. (See photo H56.)

Row 3—Pattern shed. Pick up right selvage as you insert batten. Split and twist selvage on right. With wool yarn pass over first four warps and first pair on front of batten. With right hand pick up first and second pair and pass yarn in back, thus wrapping around the first pair. Pick up second and third pair and pass yarn in back, thus wrapping around the second pair. Proceed across warp ending with passing in front of last four warps and through split selvage. Remove batten.

Row 4—Pull shed. Insert batten and beat. Split and twist selvage on right same as for Row 3. Weave with fine cotton. Beat with batten and remove. Beat with comb and then push weft down with pointed stick. Continue as established for ½ ″.

Note: You do not beat in pattern shed. Beat only when you are weaving with fine cotton. In these sheds you beat very hard after you insert the batten, you weave with the cotton, then you beat again with batten. Remove batten and beat with the comb, then push weft down around the wrap areas with pointed stick.

It is worth mentioning that the Hopi weavers keep their batten flat in the shed when wrapping with the wool yarn.

Good Weaving Habits—In weaving pattern right to left, pick up pairs of warps with your left hand and with your right hand roll the butterfly in a vertical position in back of these pairs. Don't switch the butterfly from one hand to the other; that is wasted motion. In weaving pattern left to right, you pick up with your right hand and roll the butterfly with your left hand. After each roll, pull butterfly down so weft is kept close to weaving line. (See photos H57 and H58.) This may seem awkward in the beginning but persevere and you will master it.

From here on we will give you only necessary details. You should know how to handle the beating, selvage, etc.

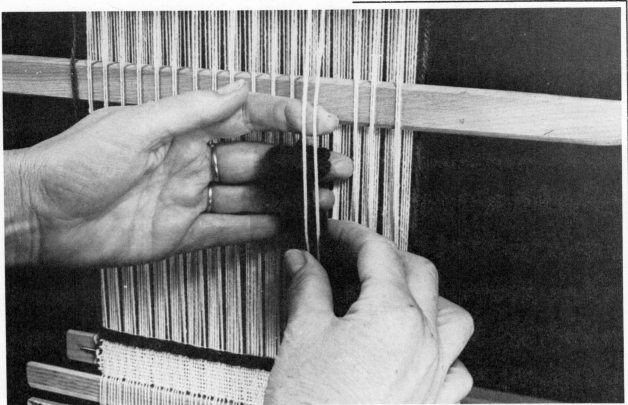

Photo H57. When weaving right to left, pick up warp pairs with left hand and holding butterfly in a vertical position, roll butterfly behind pairs with right hand.

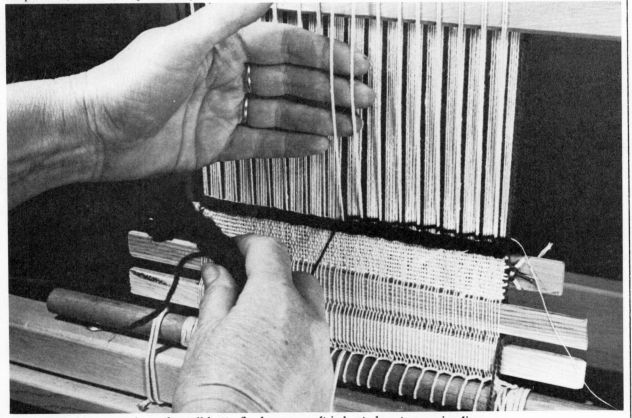

Photo H58. After wrap is made, pull butterfly down so weft is kept close to weaving line.

Change of Pattern — Vertical Lines

Row 1—Pattern shed. Pick up first pair and weave in back of it. Pick up first, second and third pairs and weave. You have wrapped first pair. Pick up third, fourth and fifth and weave. Wrapped third pair. Pick up fifth, sixth and seventh and weave. Wrapped fifth pair. Continue across wrapping every other pair and skipping behind every other pair. When row is complete, the uneven pairs are wrapped and the even pairs are showing up white.

Row 2—Weave with fine cotton.

Row 3—Pattern shed. Same as Row 1 in reverse direction.

Row 4—Weave with fine cotton.

Continue as established for ½ ". End with both wefts on right.

It's time to raise your stretcher before continuing.

Now change your pattern by wrapping around the ones you didn't wrap in preceding area and go behind the ones you wrapped in preceding area. Continue for ½ ". You now know how to make thin vertical white lines. (See photo H59.)

Photo H59. Bottom to top:
    Plain embroidery weave
    Vertical lines
    Squares
    On right: Fastening in new weft by pushing end into pattern pocket with toothpick.
    Pick-up made for pattern without wrapping

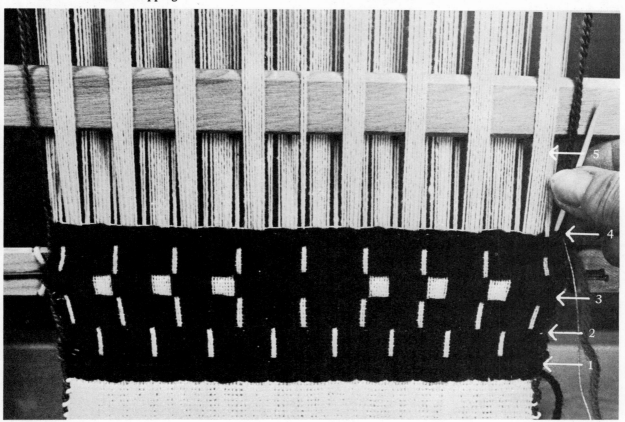

Change of Pattern — Squares

Row 1—Pattern shed. Take wool weft behind right selvage threads, over first four warps and the first pair on batten, pick up first and second pairs and weave. Pick up second and third pairs plus all warps in between and weave. Pick up third and fourth pairs and weave. Pick up fourth and fifth pairs plus all warps in between and weave. Pick up fifth and sixth pairs and weave. Pick up sixth and seventh pairs and all warps in between and weave. Pick up seventh and eighth and weave. Pick up eighth and ninth and weave. Pick up ninth and tenth and weave. Pick up tenth and eleventh and weave. Pick up eleventh and twelfth and all warps in between and weave. Pick up twelfth and thirteenth and weave. Pick up thirteenth and fourteenth and all in between and weave. Pick up fourteenth and fifteenth and weave. Pick up fifteenth and sixteenth and all in between and weave. Pick up sixteenth and seventeenth and weave. Pick up seventeenth and weave out through the split selvage.

The rule to remember is: When you want an area to weave white, you take the weft behind it as you weave. You can go behind any warps you wish to develop design. Continue as established for ½″, then repeat the preceding vertical stripe area and then the plain embroidery area, as you began.

Tension of Weft

The tension of the wool weft should be not tight or loose but a happy medium. If you pull it tight, your fabric will draw in too much. If you have it too loose, the wool will hang away from the fabric when off the loom. A little experimentation will help you decide the correct tension on the wool weft.

Tension on the fine white yarn should not be so great that it draws in the fabric. Think loose rather than tight.

Pattern without Wrapping

The next pattern change does not involve wrapping. You can skip your wool weft through the warp as you wish without wrapping around any pairs. For example:

Row 1—Pick up right selvage with batten, then pick up first, third, fifth and seventh groups of eight warps that fall between the pairs. Pick up ninth pair, then the tenth, twelfth, fourteenth and sixteenth groups of eight. Weave. (See photo H 59.) Continue this sequence of pick-up for four pattern rows, ending with both wefts on right.

Row 9—Pick up right selvage with batten and all pairs plus first, third, fifth, seventh, tenth, twelfth, fourteenth and sixteenth groups of eight. Continue this sequence of pick-up for four pattern rows. Then repeat the first sequence of pick-up again for four pattern rows.

Combining Preceding Techniques to Create Diamond Design

(Detail for pattern rows only.)

Rows 1, 2, 3 and 4—Plain embroidery weave wrapping all pairs and covering all warps.

Pattern row 5—Weft on right. Skip over 4, pick up first pair plus 2 (4 ends), skip 6, wrap second pair, *skip 6, pick up 6, skip 6, wrap 2. Repeat from * across warp ending with pick up 4, skip 4.

Pattern row 6—Skip over 4, pick 6, *skip 4, wrap 2, skip 4, pick 10. Repeat from * across warp ending with pick 6, skip 4.

Pattern row 7—Skip 4, pick 8, *skip 2, wrap 2, skip 2, pick 14. Repeat from * across warp ending with pick 8, skip 4.

Pattern row 8—Skip 4, pick 10, wrap 2, *pick 8, wrap 2. Repeat from * across warp ending with pick 10, skip 4. In this row you are skipping behind all the large groups and wrapping all the pairs.

Repeat rows 7, 6, 5, 4, 3, 2 and 1. (See photo H60.)

Photo H60. Bottom to top:
    Vertical lines
    Pattern without wrapping
    Combining techniques for
       diamond design
    Two Hopi type designs

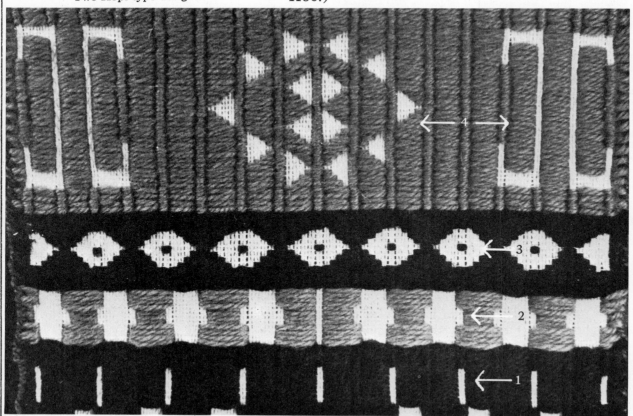

Use your pointed stick to help find the right warp threads. As you pick them up, slip them over the batten. After you have completed the pick-up, check the warps on front of batten to be sure you have them correct before you begin to weave and wrap.

You now have the knowledge to develop any design you wish with the embroidery weave. Continue pattern weaving for another 3″ or 4″.

Working with Two Colors

To enhance your designs you may wish to use two colors of wool weft in each row of design. To do this easily carry one color on the back; that is, bring the new color from back to front, weave, then finish with that color by taking it to the back. The regular pattern wool yarn will weave from edge to edge skipping across in back of the second color area. If your design in the middle is very large, it would be wise to use several wefts rather than have one skipping in too long a length across the back. (See photo H61.)

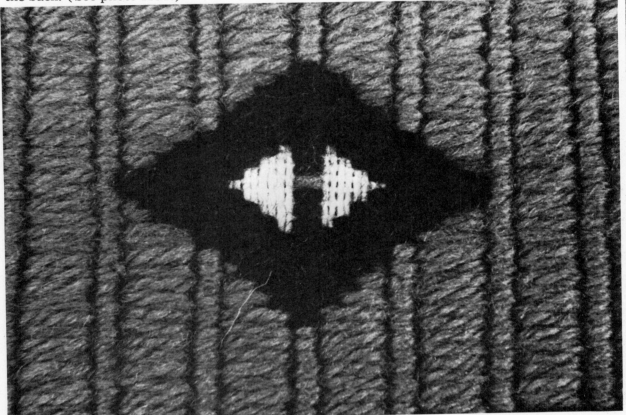

Photo H61. Two-color technique. Background color skips behind diamond design.

After the pattern area is completed, remove the pattern heddle stick and continue plain weave with the heavy cotton. Refer to Finishing the Rug (page 66). The same rules apply more or less for the last few inches of your sash weaving.

When weaving is completed, refer to Removing Rug from Loom (page 74). The same rules apply.

The Finishing Touches for Your Sash

If you have any loose ends of weft, work them

into the weaving. You should have fastened most of them as described earlier.

To complete the fringe, twist two loop ends separately in one direction, then together in opposite direction and tie knot in end. Refer to Finishing the Fringe (Hopi Belt section, page 138). This is the way our instructor demonstrates. However, many sash fringes are not finished as well. Some weavers just take the looped warp and knot it close to the weaving. They use a square knot. Some sashes have every loop knotted while others have every tenth pair of loops knotted.

You have completed one-half of a sash. You should weave another piece exactly the same and sew them together at the plain ends.

There is no set way to sew them together. I find that an overcast stitch is used often. It is sewn very loosely so ends just touch when the two pieces are laid out flat. The yarn the Hopi use to sew the two pieces together is sometimes the same heavy white cotton they wove with. If the twining cord was not in color to match the selvage cords, then they often used a red yarn to sew with to achieve color across the end.

When Problems Develop

We have covered this quite thoroughly in preceding chapters on rug and belt weaving. If a problem develops, review the chapters and find the information that will help you. Problems in weaving are basically the same no matter what you are working on. Often all it takes is just a little common sense to find the solution.

Source of Supplies

Loom rods and items for Hopi-type loom
The Pendleton Ship
Box 233 Jordon Road
Sedona, Arizona 86336

Battens and combs (forks)
Gillans's Specialties
P.O. Box 633
Solana Beach, California 92075

Living Designs
313 South Murphy Avenue
Sunnyvale, California 94086

The Pendleton Shop

Occasionally can be found at trading posts on the reservation

Warp and weft yarns for Hopi weaving
The Pendleton Shop

Most knitting shops

Spindles—Hopi type
The Pendleton Shop

Books on Hopi Weaving
Craft & Hobby Book Service
P.O. Box 626
Pacific Grove, California 93950
The Pendleton Shop

Further Reading

Book of the Hopi by Frank Waters and White Bear Fredericks (New York: The Viking Press, Inc., 1963).

North American Indian Arts by Andrew H. Whiteford (New York: Golden Press, 1970).

Pueblo Crafts by Ruth Underhill (Lawrence, Kan.: Haskell Institute, 1944).

Index